10 COOK POTATOES

AMRITA S. PRIYA

JAICO PUBLISHING HOUSE

Ahmedabad Bangalore Bhopal Chennai
Delhi Hyderabad Kolkata Mumbai

Published by Jaico Publishing House
121 Mahatma Gandhi Road
Mumbai - 400 001
jaicopub@vsnl.com
www.jaicobooks.com

© Amrita S. Priya

100 WAYS TO COOK POTATOES
ISBN 978-81-7992-710-6

First Jaico Impression: 2007
Second Jaico Impression: 2008

No part of this book may be reproduced or utilized in
any form or by any means, electronic or
mechanical including photocopying, recording or by
any information storage and retrieval system,
without permission in writing from the publishers.

Printed by Pashupati Printers (P) Ltd., Delhi-95

Dedication

To my husband who is my pillar of strength and to my parents to whom I want to prove that all their efforts in bringing me up has not been futile.

Acknowledgements

Cooking and writing have been the only two passions of my life. I have been writing recipe columns in newspapers. So writing this cookery book would not have been possible without the experience of writing recipe columns.

While writing this book, I have consulted Mrs. Manju Sinha, my mother who has given me very valuable inputs and who is the one who is most excited to see this book in print. I am extremely grateful to her for everything.

I would like to thank Mrs. Varinder Kaur for her genuine interest in my work, practical suggestions and advice regarding a few recipes.

My thanks go to my sister for bearing all my boring discussions and stimulating me with her constructive and critical comments.

Once upon a time, my brother loved only potatoes and indulgently gorged on the delicious varieties of potato I experimented for him. The root of the idea to think about different ways to cook potatoes lies here. So I want to thank him for being like that when I was developing the techniques of cooking.

I cannot neglect the encouraging words of all those who love the food I cook. Their praises are the backbone of my endeavours.

I want to thank Medhaa, who at such a tender age has been generous enough to let me devote time to produce this piece. Without her co-operation this book was not possible.

Contents

Introduction		viii
1.	Potato Tikki	1
2.	Bharwan Aloo	2
3.	Aloo Paratha	3
4.	Nonbari	4
5.	Aloo Posto	5
6.	Aloo Bhaja	6
7.	Moru Kulambu	7
8.	Aloo Chaat	8
9.	Aloo Pakora	10
10.	Finger Chips	11
11.	Aloo Poha	12
12.	Baked Potatoes	13
13.	Potato Bharta	14
14.	Aloo Raita	15
15.	Potato Salad	16
16.	Aloo Kachumbar	17
17.	Potato Fried Rice	18
18.	Batata Vada	19
19.	Bhaji	20
20.	Potato Sandwich	21
21.	Stuffed Pakora	22
22.	Bread Chop	23
23.	Potato in Mustard Gravy	24
24.	Potato in Coriander Gravy	25
25.	Potato in Tomato Gravy	26
26.	Yogurt Potato	27
27.	Aloo Palak	28
28.	Aloo Methi	29
29.	Aloo Matar	30
30.	Potato Stuffing in Bitter Gourd	31
31.	Potato Biryani	32

32.	Aloo Chana	34
33.	Aloo Chane Ki Dal	35
34.	Aloo Kachalu	36
35.	Aloo Kulcha	37
36.	Potatoes stuffed in puris	38
37.	Aloo Litti	39
38.	Potato Roll	40
39.	Potato Fritters	41
40.	Potato Chilli	42
41.	Potato Tehri	43
42.	Aloo Paneer	44
43.	Aloo Ambat	45
44.	Stuffed Tikkis	46
45.	Potato Sago	47
46.	Aloo Dum	48
47.	Aloo Khichri	49
48.	Potato Bonda	50
49.	Pav Bhaji	51
50.	Potato Patties	52
51.	Cashew Potato Curry	53
52.	Potato Cashew Fry	54
53.	Potato Toast	55
54.	Potatoes with Coconut	56
55.	Aloo Puri	57
56.	Samosa	58
57.	Potato Snackies	60
58.	Stuffed Capsicums	61
59.	Potato Kofta	62
60.	Masala Dosa	63
61.	Aloo Ka Salan	64
62.	Sweet Parathas	65
63.	Potato Halwa	66
64.	Masala Muri	67
65.	Peanuts and Potato	68
66.	Baked Cutlets in Gravy	69

67.	Potatoes in Sesame Seeds	70
68.	Aloo Salad	71
69.	Potato Pickle	72
70.	Potato Pancake	73
71.	Stuffed Puris	74
72.	Stuffed Chila	75
73.	Omelets with Potato Stuffing	76
74.	Shallow Fried Potatoes	77
75.	Potato Soup	78
76.	Milk and Cream Potato	79
77.	Healthy Potato	80
78.	Potato Chicken	81
79.	Potato Fish	82
80.	Potato Spread	83
81.	Potato Pudding	84
82.	Honey Potato	85
83.	Tea Flavored Potatoes	86
84.	Potatoes and Eggs	87
85.	Potato and Fish Cutlets	88
86.	Stuffed Eggs	89
87.	Potato Pizzas	90
88.	Biscuit Chaat	91
89.	Potato Kebabs	92
90.	Coriander Flavored Potato Tikka	93
91.	Potato Rice	94
92.	Stuffed Tomatoes	95
93.	Vermicelli Potato	96
94.	Potato and Cream Balls	97
95.	Potato Crispies	98
96.	Kashmiri Aloo	99
97.	Jhuri bhaja	100
98.	Fried Potatoes with Rice	101
99.	Potato Butter Masala	102
100.	Potato Kulhey	103

Introduction

It is difficult to neglect the global value of potato. Potato is the most common vegetable and is loved in every part of the world. We have taken it for granted but it is the fourth most important food crop of the world after wheat, rice and maize and can be afforded even by the poor. It is popular everywhere irrespective of place, status or age and therefore has a very strong mass as well as class appeal.

Potato has innumerable varieties and virtues. It is rich in carbohydrates, minerals and vitamins. Though everyone loves potato, they have limited knowledge about its culinary versatility.

This book aims to make you aware of how your favorite vegetable can be cooked in a variety of ways. So instead of serving this highly nutritious food in the same old boring style, try out the recipes of this book and make your meals more interesting.

For your convenience, I have structured the recipes in a very easy to follow format. Nutritional analysis follows each recipe to give you an idea of the nutritional value of the dish you are preparing. I have tried to use as little oil as possible, but you can add more oil or spices to the dishes according to your taste. With my ideas and your adaptations and perseverance be assured of success in whatever you cook from this book.

Happy cooking!

1. *Potato Tikki*

Number of Serving: 6

Ingredients

4 large, boiled potatoes
¼ cup finely chopped onion
2 chopped green chillies
¼ cup chopped coriander leaves
Salt to taste
1 teaspoon white pepper
2 tablespoons peanut oil

Method

- Peel and grate the potatoes.
- Add all the ingredients except oil and mix well.
- Divide into 6 equal portions. Make balls and then press gently between the palms.
- Preheat a non-stick griddle over high heat. Place the potato tikkis on it.
- Drizzle 1 tablespoon oil at the sides of the potato tikkis. Cook till one side gets reddish brown.
- Turn all of them to the other side. Drizzle remaining oil and cook till the other side turns brown. Serve piping hot.

Nutritive value per serving

ENERGY	FAT	CHO	C.H	FIBRE	PROTEIN	CALCIUM	IRON	VIT C
Kcal	Gm	Mg	Gm	Gm	Gm	Mg	Mg	Mg
201	11	3	26	3	3	57	1	52

2. Bharwan Aloo

Number of servings: 4

Ingredients

4 medium sized potatoes
1 tablespoon coriander powder
2 dry red chillies
1 tablespoon dry pomegranate seeds
½ tablespoon turmeric powder
½ tablespoon salt
water
½ cup yogurt
A drop of edible orange color (optional)

Method

- Peel the potatoes.
- Wash and slit ¾ of each potato.
- Dry roast red chillies for two minutes on a griddle over high heat. Grind along with the pomegranate seeds without using any water.
- Add turmeric powder, salt and coriander powder. Make a paste using a little water.
- Stuff equal portions into the potatoes. Seal by tying with string so that the filling does not spill out.
- Whip the yogurt. Add a pinch of salt and edible color. Marinate the potatoes in it for 20 minutes.
- Grill in a preheated oven till the potatoes turn reddish brown and tender. Remove the strings before serving.

Nutritive value per serving

ENERGY	FAT	CHO	C.H	FIBRE	PROTEIN	CALCIUM	IRON	VIT C
Kcal	Gm	Mg	Gm	Gm	Gm	Mg	Mg	Mg
262	8	26	39	8	11	113	6	27

3. *Aloo Paratha*

Number of Serving: 6

Ingredients

3½ cups wheat flour
water
4 boiled potatoes
10 tablespoons peanut oil
¼ cup chopped onion
2 chopped green chillies
¼ cup chopped coriander leaves
Salt to taste.

Method

- Knead wheat flour with water.
- Peel and grate the potatoes.
- Preheat 2 tablespoons oil over high heat. Add onion and green chillies and fry till onions turn golden brown.
- Add grated potatoes, coriander leaves and salt. Fry for 2 minutes. Remove from fire.
- Divide the kneaded flour into 8 equal portions and make balls.
- Dust the balls with a little flour. Flatten between palms into 2 inches diameter round discs.
- Place a portion of the potato filling in the middle of one of the discs, enfold and properly seal the edges.
- Place on a preheated griddle and half bake over high heat, turning over once.
- Add 1 tablespoon peanut oil and shallow fry both the sides until golden brown, approximately 3-5 minutes.
- Repeat process for the remaining balls and potato filling.

Nutritive value per serving

ENERGY	FAT	CHO	C H	FIBRE	PROTEIN	CALCIUM	IRON	VIT C
Kcal	Gm	Mg	Gm	Gm	Gm	Mg	Mg	Mg
447	22	2	58	9	10	60	3	39

4. *Nonbari*

Number of servings: 12

Ingredients

1 potato
1 inch chopped ginger
2 chopped green chillies
Salt to taste
1½ cups wheat flour
water
1 cup peanut oil

Method

- Peel and finely chop potatoes.
- Add potato, ginger, green chilli and salt to the wheat flour.
- Add water and mix well. The paste should be of dropping consistency.
- Preheat oil in a deep frying pan over high heat
- Drop in 4 - 5 tablespoons of the paste and deep fry over medium heat till the nonbaris turn golden brown
- Repeat process for the remaining mixture, dropping in 4 -5 tablespoons in one batch. Serve hot.

Nutritive value per serving

ENERGY	FAT	CHO	C.H	FIBRE	PROTEIN	CALCIUM	IRON	VIT C
Kcal	Gm	Mg	Gm	Gm	Gm	Mg	Mg	Mg
116	6	0	14	2	2	8	1	20

Note – approximately, only 1/3 cup peanut oil will get used.

5. *Aloo Posto*

Number of servings: 2

Ingredients

2 potatoes
½ cup poppy seeds
1 dry red chilli
3½ tablespoons mustard oil
1 chopped onion
1 teaspoon garlic paste
1 teaspoon ginger paste
Salt to taste
1 teaspoon sugar (optional)
1 teaspoon turmeric powder
2 slit green chillies

Method

- Peel and chop potatoes.
- Grind poppy seeds and dry red chilli into a smooth paste using a little water.
- Preheat 3 tablespoons oil in a small frying pan.
- Add chopped onions and fry till golden brown.
- Add chopped potatoes. Fry for 2 minutes. Add garlic and ginger pastes, salt, sugar and turmeric powder.
- Cover and cook till potatoes are done. Add the poppy seed paste, slit green chillies and remaining oil.
- Cook over high heat for 3 minutes and serve with cooked rice.

Nutritive value per serving

ENERGY	FAT	CHO	C.H	FIBRE	PROTEIN	CALCIUM	IRON	VIT C
Kcal	Gm	Mg	Gm	Gm	Gm	Mg	Mg	Mg
555	40	0	44	8	11	549	6	210

6. Aloo Bhaja

Number of servings: 2

Ingredients

2 potatoes, peeled and cut in thin stripes
½ tablespoon of salt
1 teaspoon turmeric powder
1 teaspoon red chilli powder
2 ½ tablespoons mustard oil

Method

- Wash the potatoes and add salt, turmeric powder and chilli powder.
- Set aside for twenty minutes.
- Preheat oil in a small frying pan over high heat and fry the potatoes till they get tender.

Nutritive value per serving

ENERGY	FAT	CHO	C.H	FIBRE	PROTEIN	CALCIUM	IRON	VIT C
Kcal	Gm	Mg	Gm	Gm	Gm	Mg	Mg	Mg
252	17	0	23	2	3	21	1	28

7. *Moru Kulambu*

Number of servings 2

Ingredients

2 teaspoons split yellow peas
2 cups water
2 green chillies
1 teaspoon coriander seeds
1 teaspoon cumin seeds
3 tablespoons grated fresh coconut
3 medium sized boiled potatoes
1½ cups sour yogurt
Salt to taste
¼ teaspoon turmeric powder
1 tablespoon peanut oil
½ teaspoon black mustard seeds
½ teaspoon fenugreek seeds
2 red chilies
6 curry leaves

Method

- Soak split yellow peas in ½ cup water for half an hour.
- Drain away water and grind yellow peas with green chillies, coriander seeds, cumin seeds, and grated coconut using 4 tablespoons water.
- Peel and cut each potato into four pieces.
- Whip yogurt and transfer to a medium saucepan. Add remaining water, salt, turmeric powder, ground paste and potato pieces.
- Cook over medium heat till desired consistency. Set aside.
- Preheat oil in a small frying pan.
- Add mustard seeds, fenugreek seeds, dry red chillies and curry leaves.
- Saute for two minutes and add to the cooked potato. Serve with steamed rice.

Nutritive value per serving

ENERGY	FAT	CHO	C.H	FIBRE	PROTEIN	CALCIUM	IRON	VIT C
Kcal	Gm	Mg	Gm	Gm	Gm	Mg	Mg	Mg
431	17	23	60	6	14	284	4	292

8. *Aloo Chaat*

Number of servings: 4

Ingredients

Lemon sized tamarind
1/3 cup water
4 tablespoons sugar
4 large, boiled potatoes
½ cup finely chopped onion
2 green chillies
Salt to taste
1 teaspoon white pepper
2 tablespoons peanut oil
2 cups whipped yogurt
¼ teaspoon rock salt
½ teaspoon red chilli powder
1 tablespoon cumin powder
¼ cup chopped coriander leaves

Method

- Soak tamarind in water for half an hour. Remove the pulp and strain. Add sugar and red chilli powder. Mix the sugar with spoon so that it dissolves properly. Set aside.
- Peel the potatoes and mash properly.
- Add ¼ cup onion, green chillies, salt and pepper. Mix well.
- Divide into 4 equal portions. Make balls and then press gently between the palms.
- Preheat a non-stick griddle over high heat. Place the potatoes on it.
- Drizzle 1 tablespoon oil at the sides of the potatoes. Cook till one side of the potatoes gets reddish brown.
- Turn all of them to the other side. Drizzle remaining oil and cook till the other side turns brown.
- Remove from fire and transfer to 4 different plates. Press lightly with the hand.

- Whip the yogurt and add rock salt.
- Pour equally over the potatoes.
- Add the tamarind syrup and cumin powder. Garnish with the remaining onion and coriander leaves.

Nutritive value per serving

ENERGY	FAT	CHO	C.H	FIBRE	PROTEIN	CALCIUM	IRON	VIT C
Kcal	Gm	Mg	Gm	Gm	Gm	Mg	Mg	Mg
450	20	20	63	6	9	253	3	25

9. *Aloo Pakora*

Number of servings: 24

Ingredients

4 potatoes
1½ cups gram flour
water
½ teaspoon turmeric powder
½ teaspoon pepper
Salt to taste
1 cup oil

Method

- Peel and cut potatoes into roundels (approx 6 roundels of 1 potato)
- Make a thick batter of gram flour and water. Add turmeric powder, pepper and salt.
- Preheat oil in a small frying pan over high heat.
- Dip each roundel into the gram flour paste and deep fry till golden brown. Serve piping hot.

Nutritive value per serving

ENERGY	FAT	CHO	C.H	FIBRE	PROTEIN	CALCIUM	IRON	VIT C
Kcal	Gm	Mg	Gm	Gm	Gm	Mg	Mg	Mg
104	7	0	10	1	1	3	1	4

Note – approximately, only ¾ cup peanut oil will get used.

10. *Finger Chips*

Number of servings: 4

Ingredients

4 large potatoes
1 cup peanut oil
Salt to taste
White pepper to taste

Method

- Cut the potatoes into finger size pieces.
- Preheat oil in a medium frying pan over high heat.
- Fry the potato pieces over high heat in 2-3 batches till they get tender.
- Drain excess oil on the kitchen paper. Add salt and pepper. Serve hot.

Nutritive value per serving

ENERGY	FAT	CHO	C.H	FIBRE	PROTEIN	CALCIUM	IRON	VIT C
Kcal	Gm	Mg	Gm	Gm	Gm	Mg	Mg	Mg
335	27	0	22	2	3	9	1	24

Note – approximately, only ½ cup peanut oil will get used.

11. *Aloo Poha*

Number of servings: 2

Ingredients

2 potatoes
1 onion
2 green chillies
3 tablespoons peanut oil
1 tablespoon cumin seeds
3 cups pressed rice
Salt to taste
Pepper to taste
½ cup chopped coriander leaves

Method

- Peel and finely chop the potatoes. Chop the onion and green chillies.
- Soak pressed rice in water and completely drain away the water after 1 minute.
- Preheat oil in a medium frying pan over high heat.
- Add cumin seeds. After a minute add onion and fry for 2 minutes.
- Add potatoes and green chillies and fry till potatoes are tender.
- Add pressed rice, salt and pepper to the potatoes. Fry for 5 minutes over high heat.
- Garnish with coriander leaves and serve.

Nutritive value per serving

ENERGY	FAT	CHO	C.H	FIBRE	PROTEIN	CALCIUM	IRON	VIT C
Kcal	Gm	Mg	Gm	Gm	Gm	Mg	Mg	Mg
495	22	0	70	5	9	149	9	197

12. *Baked Potatoes*

Number of servings: 8

Ingredients

4 large, boiled potatoes
Salt to taste
White Pepper to taste
½ tablespoon peanut oil
2 cups grated cheese

Method

- Peel and grate the potatoes. Add salt and pepper.
- Grease a baking tray with the peanut oil. Spread potatoes evenly.
- Spread the grated cheese over the potatoes and cook over a preheated oven for around 10 minutes over 375 degrees. Cut into 8 equal portions and serve.

Nutritive value per serving

ENERGY	FAT	CHO	C H	FIBRE	PROTEIN	CALCIUM	IRON	VIT C
Kcal	Gm	Mg	Gm	Gm	Gm	Mg	Mg	Mg
119	5	2	18	2	2	27	trace	6

13. *Potato Bharta*

Number of servings: 2

Ingredients

2 large, boiled potatoes
1 small onion, chopped
1 chopped green chilli
1 teaspoon mustard oil
½ cup chopped coriander leaves
Salt to taste

Method

- Peel and mash the potatoes. Add all the ingredients.

Nutritive value per serving

ENERGY	FAT	CHO	C.H	FIBRE	PROTEIN	CALCIUM	IRON	VIT C
Kcal	Gm	Mg	Gm	Gm	Gm	Mg	Mg	Mg
293	12	4	46	6	7	159	4	112

14. *Aloo Raita*

Number of servings: 4

Ingredients

4 boiled potatoes
2 cups whipped yogurt
Salt to taste
¼ teaspoon rock salt
½ tablespoon cumin powder
½ teaspoon red chilli powder
¼ cup chopped coriander leaves

Method

- Peel and chop the potatoes.
- Transfer yogurt to a big bowl. Add salt, rock salt, cumin powder, red chilli powder and coriander leaves.
- Add potatoes and serve chilled.

Nutritive value per serving

ENERGY	FAT	CHO	C.H	FIBRE	PROTEIN	CALCIUM	IRON	VIT C
Kcal	Gm	Mg	Gm	Gm	Gm	Mg	Mg	Mg
132	4	16	18	1	6	183	2	23

15. *Potato Salad*

Number of servings: 2

Ingredients

2 boiled potatoes
Salt to taste
White Pepper to taste
1 teaspoon olive oil

Method

- Peel and cut the potatoes into roundels.
- Add all the ingredients.

Nutritive value per serving

ENERGY	FAT	CHO	C.H	FIBRE	PROTEIN	CALCIUM	IRON	VIT C
Kcal	Gm	Mg	Gm	Gm	Gm	Mg	Mg	Mg
116	2	0	22	2	3	9	1	24

16. Aloo Kachumbar

Number of servings: 2

Ingredients

2 boiled potatoes
1 onion
1 tomato
Salt to taste
¼ lemon
¼ teaspoon chilli powder

Method

- Peel and cut potatoes, onion and tomato into cubes.
- Add salt, lemon juice and chilli powder.

Nutritive value per serving

ENERGY	FAT	CHO	C.H	FIBRE	PROTEIN	CALCIUM	IRON	VIT C
Kcal	Gm	Mg	Gm	Gm	Gm	Mg	Mg	Mg
133	trace	0	50	4	4	25	1	43

17. Potato Fried Rice

Number of servings: 1

Ingredients

1 cup rice
1 potato
1 teaspoon peanut oil
½ teaspoon cumin seeds
Salt to taste
Pepper to taste
2 cups water

Method

- Wash the rice. Peel and cut the potato into 4 pieces.
- Preheat oil in a pressure cooker over high heat.
- Add cumin seeds. After a minute add potatoes and fry for 5 minutes.
- Add rice and fry for 3 minutes. Add salt, pepper and water and close the lid of the pressure cooker and cook over high heat till one whistle.
- Open the lid of the pressure cooker after all the air escapes and serve.

Nutritive value per serving

ENERGY	FAT	CHO	C.H	FIBRE	PROTEIN	CALCIUM	IRON	VIT C
Kcal	Gm	Mg	Gm	Gm	Gm	Mg	Mg	Mg
815	6	0	170	4	16	79	10	24

18. *Batata Vada*

Number of servings: 8

Ingredients

1 ½ cups gram flour
½ teaspoon coriander seeds
½ teaspoon turmeric powder
1 teaspoon salt
½ teaspoon red chilli powder
water
A pinch of soda bi carbonate
4 boiled potatoes
1 teaspoon garam masala
2 tablespoons chopped coriander leaves
½ teaspoon pomegranate seeds
8 blanched cashew nuts
½ lemon
¼ teaspoon sugar
1 cup peanut oil for deep-frying

Method

- Add coriander seeds, turmeric powder, ½ teaspoon salt and ¼ teaspoon red chilli powder to the gram flour. Make a batter using water. Add soda bi carbonate. Set aside.
- Peel and mash the potatoes and add ½ teaspoon salt, ¼ teaspoon red chilli powder garam masala, coriander leaves, pomegranate seeds, cashew nuts, lemon juice and sugar.
- Divide the potatoes into 8 equal portions. Make balls.
- Preheat oil in a medium sized frying pan over high heat.
- Dip the potato balls in the batter and deep fry 4 at a time over medium heat till they turn golden brown. Serve hot.

Nutritive value per serving

ENERGY	FAT	CHO	C.H	FIBRE	PROTEIN	CALCIUM	IRON	VIT C
Kcal	Gm	Mg	Gm	Gm	Gm	Mg	Mg	Mg
1070	81	2	74	11	26	96	7	11

Note – approximately, only ½ cup peanut oil will get used.

19. *Bhaji*

Number of servings: 4

Ingredients

4 boiled potatoes
2 tablespoons peanut oil
1 teaspoon cumin seed
1 teaspoon black mustard
1 chopped onion
2 chopped green chillies
1 chopped tomato
½ teaspoon garlic paste
1 tablespoon coconut paste
4 garlic cloves
Salt to taste
1 tablespoon turmeric powder

Method

- Peel and cut the potatoes into 4 pieces each, lengthwise.
- Preheat oil in a medium frying pan over high heat.
- Add cumin seeds and mustard and sauté for a minute.
- Add onions and green chillies and fry for three minutes.
- Add tomatoes and fry for another two minutes.
- Add garlic paste, coconut paste and slit garlic cloves. Fry over low heat till tomatoes reduce to a thick paste, approximately 5-6 minutes.
- Add potatoes, salt and turmeric powder. Stir-fry over high heat for 5 minutes.

Nutritive value per serving

ENERGY	FAT	CHO	C.H	FIBRE	PROTEIN	CALCIUM	IRON	VIT C
Kcal	Gm	Mg	Gm	Gm	Gm	Mg	Mg	Mg
204	8	0	31	4	4	38	3	88

20. *Potato Sandwich*

Number of servings: 4

Ingredients

2 tablespoons peanut oil
1 chopped onion
¼ cup green peas
2 boiled potatoes
Salt to taste
Pepper to taste
4 bread slices

Method

- Preheat oil in a small frying pan over high heat.
- Add onion and fry till they get transparent.
- Add green peas and fry till they get tender.
- Peel and mash the potatoes and add along with salt and pepper. Fry for 5 minutes. Remove from fire.
- Divide the potatoes into 4 equal portions. Cut each bread slice into 2 triangular pieces. Stuff each portion of potato between 2 triangular pieces of bread. Grill. Serve hot.

Nutritive value per serving

ENERGY	FAT	CHO	C.H	FIBRE	PROTEIN	CALCIUM	IRON	VIT C
Kcal	Gm	Mg	Gm	Gm	Gm	Mg	Mg	Mg
256	12	2	34	4	5	62	1	12

21. Stuffed Pakora

Number of servings: 4

Ingredients

2 boiled potatoes
1 cup peanut oil
1 onion, chopped
¼ cup green peas
Salt to taste
Pepper to taste
4 bread slices
¾ cup gram flour
½ teaspoon turmeric powder
water

Method

- Peel and mash the potatoes.
- Preheat 2 tablespoons oil in a small frying pan over high heat. Add the onion and fry till they get transparent.
- Add green peas and fry till they get tender.
- Add potatoes, salt and pepper. Fry for 5 minutes. Remove from fire. Divide into 4 equal portions.
- Cut each bread slice into 2 pieces (either in triangular or rectangular shape)
- Stuff each portion of fried potatoes between two pieces of bread.
- Add salt and turmeric powder to the gram flour. Make batter using water.
- Preheat oil in a small frying pan over high heat. Dip one of the stuffed bread cutlets in the gram flour batter.
- Deep fry till golden brown. Repeat process for the remaining 3 stuffed bread cutlets.

Nutritive value per serving

ENERGY	FAT	CHO	C.H	FIBRE	PROTEIN	CALCIUM	IRON	VIT C
Kcal	Gm	Mg	Gm	Gm	Gm	Mg	Mg	Mg
448	24	2	53	5	8	69	2	15

Note – approximately, only 1/3 cup peanut oil will get used.

22. Bread Chop

Number of servings: 4

Ingredients

2 boiled potatoes

1 cup peanut oil

1 chopped onion

¼ cup green peas

Salt to taste

Pepper to taste

4 bread slices

Method

- Peel and mash the potatoes.
- Preheat 2 tablespoons oil in a small frying pan over high heat. Add onion and fry till they get transparent.
- Add green peas and fry till they get tender.
- Add potatoes, salt and pepper. Fry for 5 minutes. Remove from fire. Divide into 4 equal portions
- Take 2 cups water in a bowl. Dip 1 slice of bread. Remove immediately. Press lightly between palms to drain away water.
- Put a portion of fried potatoes in between. Enfold and seal the edges. Give it round or oval shape. Repeat process for rest of the breads and potato.
- Preheat oil over high heat in the frying pan. Deep fry the bread chops till golden brown. Serve hot.

Nutritive value per serving

ENERGY	FAT	CHO	C.H	FIBRE	PROTEIN	CALCIUM	IRON	VIT C
Kcal	Gm	Mg	Gm	Gm	Gm	Mg	Mg	Mg
355	23	2	34	4	5	62	1	12

Note – approximately, only 1/3 cup peanut oil will get used.

23. Potato in Mustard Gravy

Number of servings: 4

Ingredients

- 4 potatoes
- 1 onion
- 1 tomato
- 2 ½ tablespoons mustard oil
- 1 teaspoon mustard seeds
- 1 tablespoon mustard paste
- 1 teaspoon turmeric powder
- 1 teaspoon coriander powder
- ½ teaspoon chilli powder
- Salt to taste
- water
- 1 teaspoon garam masala

Method

- Peel and cut potatoes into 4 pieces each. Finely chop onion and tomato.
- Preheat oil in a small pressure cooker over high heat. Add mustard seeds. After a minute add onion and fry for 3 minutes.
- Add potato and fry for another 3 minutes. Add tomato, mustard paste, turmeric powder, coriander powder, chilli powder and salt. Fry for 10 minutes over medium heat.
- Add water and garam masala and pressure cook till 1 whistle over high heat.

Nutritive value per serving

ENERGY	FAT	CHO	C.H	FIBRE	PROTEIN	CALCIUM	IRON	VIT C
Kcal	Gm	Mg	Gm	Gm	Gm	Mg	Mg	Mg
203	10	0	27	3	4	30	2	32

24. Potato in Coriander Gravy

Number of servings: 4

Ingredients

4 potatoes
1 onion
A bunch of coriander leaves
2 ½ tablespoons mustard oil
1 teaspoon coriander seeds
1 teaspoon chilli powder
1 tablespoon coriander powder
Salt to taste
¼ lemon
water
1 teaspoon garam masala

Method

- Peel and cut potatoes into 4 pieces each. Finely chop onion.
- Remove the coriander leaves from stem, wash and grind into a fine paste.
- Preheat oil in a small pressure cooker over high heat. Add coriander seeds.
- After a minute add onion and fry for 3 minutes. Add potato and fry for another 3 minutes.
- Add chilli powder, coriander powder and salt. Fry for 5 minutes over medium heat.
- Add coriander paste, lemon juice water and garam masala and pressure-cook till 1 whistle over high heat.

Nutritive value per serving

ENERGY	FAT	CHO	C.H	FIBRE	PROTEIN	CALCIUM	IRON	VIT C
Kcal	Gm	Mg	Gm	Gm	Gm	Mg	Mg	Mg
189	9	0	26	3	3	29	2	31

25. Potato in Tomato Gravy

Number of servings: 4

Ingredients

4 potatoes
1 onion
2 large tomatoes
2 ½ tablespoons mustard oil
1 teaspoon cumin seed
1 teaspoon coriander powder
1 teaspoon turmeric powder
½ teaspoon red chilli powder
1 teaspoon garlic paste
Salt to taste
water
1 teaspoon garam masala
½ cup chopped coriander leaves

Method

- Peel and cut potatoes into 4 pieces each. Finely chop onion.
- Chop tomatoes and grind into a smooth paste.
- Preheat oil in a small pressure cooker over high heat. Add cumin seeds.
- Add onion and fry for 3 minutes. Add potato and fry for another 5 minutes.
- Add coriander powder, turmeric powder, red chilli powder, garlic paste and salt. Fry for 5 minutes over medium heat.
- Add tomato paste and fry for 2 minutes over high heat. Add water and garam Masala.
- Cover the lid of the pressure cooker and cook over high heat till 1 whistle. Garnish with coriander leaves.

Nutritive value per serving

ENERGY	FAT	CHO	C.H	FIBRE	PROTEIN	CALCIUM	IRON	VIT C
Kcal	Gm	Mg	Gm	Gm	Gm	Mg	Mg	Mg
203	9	0	28	4	4	30	2	39

26. *Yogurt Potato*

Number of servings: 4

Ingredients

4 boiled potatoes
2 onions
½ cup peanut oil
1 teaspoon mustard seeds
a pinch of turmeric powder
½ teaspoon red chilli powder
1 teaspoon coriander powder
Salt to taste
1 cup yogurt

Method

- Peel and cut potatoes into 4 pieces each. Finely chop the onions.
- Preheat oil in a medium frying pan. Deep fry the onion over high heat till golden brown. Transfer to a plate.
- Remove excess oil from the frying pan leaving only 2 tablespoons oil.
- Add mustard seeds. After a minute add the potatoes and fry over high heat for 3 minutes.
- Add turmeric powder, red chilli powder, coriander powder and salt. Fry for 5 minutes.
- Transfer to a serving bowl. Whip the yogurt and add a little salt.
- Spread yogurt evenly over the potatoes. Spread fried onions over the yogurt and serve

Nutritive value per serving

ENERGY	FAT	CHO	C H	FIBRE	PROTEIN	CALCIUM	IRON	VIT C
Kcal	Gm	Mg	Gm	Gm	Gm	Mg	Mg	Mg
280	16	8	30	3	6	99	1	28

27. Aloo Palak

Number of servings: 4

Ingredients

4 boiled potatoes
1 onion
1 bunch spinach
¼ bunch fenugreek leaves
¾ cup water
Salt to taste
4 tablespoons mustard oil
2 cinnamon sticks
1 teaspoon ginger paste
1 teaspoon garlic paste
1 teaspoon coriander powder
½ teaspoon red chilli powder
1 teaspoon garam masala.

Method

- Peel the potatoes and cut into 4 pieces each. Chop the onions finely.
- Remove the spinach and fenugreek leaves from the stems. Chop and grind into a smooth paste using ¼ cup water.
- Preheat 2 tablespoons oil in a medium frying pan over high heat. Add potatoes and fry till pale brown. Set aside.
- In the same frying pan add the remaining oil. After it gets heated add cinnamon sticks
- Add onion and fry till golden brown. Add spinach and fenugreek paste, ginger paste, garlic paste, coriander powder and red chilli powder.
- Fry for five minutes over high heat. Add potatoes, garam masala and ½ cup water. Cover and cook for another 5 minutes. Add more water if a thinner gravy is required.

Nutritive value per serving

ENERGY	FAT	CHO	C.H	FIBRE	PROTEIN	CALCIUM	IRON	VIT C
Kcal	Gm	Mg	Gm	Gm	Gm	Mg	Mg	Mg
252	14	0	31	7	4	113	4	31

28. Aloo Methi

Number of servings: 4

Ingredients

4 potatoes
1 onion
1 ½ bunch fenugreek leaves
2 ½ tablespoons mustard oil
1 teaspoon cumin seeds
2 green chillies
1 teaspoon ginger paste
1 teaspoon garlic paste
1 teaspoon coriander powder
½ teaspoon red chilli powder
1 teaspoon garam masala.

Method

- Peel and chop potatoes into 8 pieces each. Finely chop the onion.
- Remove the fenugreek leaves from the stems Finely chop and wash properly.
- Preheat oil in a medium frying pan over high heat. Add cumin seeds and green chillies.
- Add potatoes and fry for 3 minutes. Add fenugreek leaves and all the remaining ingredients.
- Stir-fry for 5 minutes. Cover and cook till potatoes are tender.

Nutritive value per serving

ENERGY	FAT	CHO	C.H	FIBRE	PROTEIN	CALCIUM	IRON	VIT C
Kcal	Gm	Mg	Gm	Gm	Gm	Mg	Mg	Mg
199	9	0	28	3	4	39	2	83

29. *Aloo Matar*

Number of servings: 4

Ingredients

4 boiled potatoes
2 green chillies
1 tomato
2 ½ tablespoons mustard oil
1 teaspoon cumin seed
1 chopped onion
1 teaspoon ginger paste
1 teaspoon garlic paste
½ teaspoon turmeric powder
1 teaspoon pepper
Salt to taste

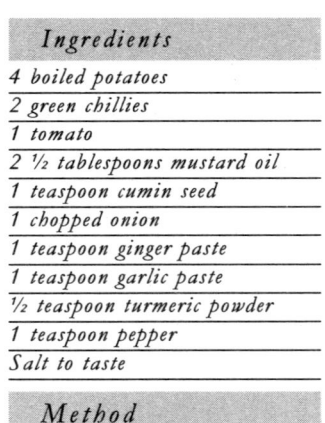

Method

- Peel and cut potatoes into 4 pieces each. Slit green chillies. Finely chop the tomato.
- Preheat oil in a small frying pan over high heat.
- Add cumin seeds and green chillies. After a minute add onion, ginger paste and garlic paste and fry till golden brown.
- Add potatoes, turmeric powder, pepper and salt. Fry for 5 minutes.
- Add green peas. Stir-fry till green peas are tender.

Nutritive value per serving

ENERGY	FAT	CHO	C.H	FIBRE	PROTEIN	CALCIUM	IRON	VIT C
Kcal	Gm	Mg	Gm	Gm	Gm	Mg	Mg	Mg
203	9	0	29	3	4	27	2	87

30. Potato Stuffing in Bitter Gourd

Number of servings:

Ingredients

2 large bitter gourds
3 medium sized boiled potatoes
1 onion
6 tablespoons mustard oil
½ teaspoon turmeric powder
Salt to taste
Juice of ½ lemon

Method

- Scrape bitter gourd. Slit around 5 inches in between and remove seeds. Smear salt all over (both inside and outside) and set aside for ½ an hour. Boil over high heat for 10 minutes. Set aside.
- Peel and mash potatoes. Finely chop the onion.
- Preheat oil in a small frying pan. Fry onion till golden brown
- Add potatoes, turmeric powder and salt and fry over high heat for 5 minutes. Add lemon juice and set aside.
- Stuff bitter gourd with fried potatoes. Tie the bitter gourd with thread so that the stuffing does not come out.
- Preheat the remaining oil in the frying pan. Fry stuffed bitter gourds till they are pale brown on all the sides. Cover and cook over low heat till gourds get cooked completely. Cut each stuffed gourd into 2 pieces with a knife.

Nutritive value per serving

ENERGY	FAT	CHO	C.H	FIBRE	PROTEIN	CALCIUM	IRON	VIT C
Kcal	Gm	Mg	Gm	Gm	Gm	Mg	Mg	Mg
414	27	3	43	4	6	149	1	54

31. *Potato Biryani*

Number of servings: 2

Ingredients

8 small potatoes (boiled)
4 tablespoons peanut oil
2 black cardamoms
2 red chillies
2 bay leaves
2 cinnamon sticks
½ cup onion paste
1 tablespoon ginger paste
1 tablespoon garlic paste
1 chopped tomato
1 teaspoon turmeric powder
1 teaspoon coriander powder
¼ teaspoon red chilli powder
Salt to taste
2 ½ cups water
1 ½ teaspoon garam masala powder
1 cup long grained rice
4 cloves
2 green cardamoms
1 tablespoon ghee
¼ cup yogurt
2 drops edible orange color (optional)

Method

- Peel the potatoes.
- Preheat oil in a medium frying pan over high heat. Fry the potatoes till they turn brown. Remove from fire.
- To the remaining oil, add black cardamoms, red chillies, 1 bay leaf and cinnamon sticks. After a minute add onion paste, ginger paste and garlic paste and fry for 3 minutes.
- Add chopped tomato, turmeric powder, coriander powder, red chilli powder and salt. Fry till the paste turns golden brown.
- Add potatoes and fry for another 5 minutes. Add ½ cup water and cover and cook till all the water dries up. Sprinkle 1 teaspoon garam masala. Set aside.

- Wash the rice and transfer to a small pressure cooker. Add 2 cups water, cloves, cardamom, 1 bay leaf and a pinch of salt. Close the lid of the pressure cooker and cook till 1 whistle. Open the lid of the pressure cooker after all the air escapes.
- Grease a heavy bottomed pan with ghee. Add a little salt and the remaining ½ teaspoon garam masala to the yogurt.
- Spread half of the cooked rice in the greased pan. Sprinkle curd over it.
- Spread the cooked potatoes over the yogurt, evenly. Cover with the remaining rice. Mix edible color with a few drops of water and sprinkle over the rice.
- Cover the lid of the pan and cook over slow flame for 5 minutes. Serve hot.

Nutritive value per serving

ENERGY	FAT	CHO	C.H	FIBRE	PROTEIN	CALCIUM	IRON	VIT C
Kcal	Gm	Mg	Gm	Gm	Gm	Mg	Mg	Mg
934	36	10	147	19	17	333	13	213

32. *Aloo Chana*

Number of servings: 4

Ingredients

1 cup boiled grams
2 boiled potatoes
2½ tablespoons mustard oil
1 teaspoon cumin seed
1 chopped onion
1 chopped tomato
1 teaspoon ginger paste
1 teaspoon garlic paste
1 teaspoon coriander powder
1 teaspoon red chilli powder
1 teaspoon turmeric powder
Salt to taste
1 cup water
1 teaspoon garam masala
¼ cup chopped coriander leaves

Method

- Soak grams in water for 4-5 hours. Drain away water and set aside.
- Peel the potatoes and cut into 4 pieces each.
- Preheat oil in a medium frying pan over high heat. Add cumin seeds.
- Add onion and fry till golden brown. Add potatoes, grams, tomato, ginger paste and garlic paste and fry for 3 minutes.
- Add coriander powder, red chilli powder, turmeric powder and salt. Fry for 10 minutes.
- Add water and garam masala. Cover and bring to boil. Garnish with coriander leaves.

Nutritive value per serving

ENERGY	FAT	CHO	C.H	FIBRE	PROTEIN	CALCIUM	IRON	VIT C
Kcal	Gm	Mg	Gm	Gm	Gm	Mg	Mg	Mg
238	12	0	29	4	6	67	3	31

33. Aloo Chane Ki Dal

Number of servings: 4

Ingredients

1 cup split skinless chickpeas
2 potatoes
2 ½ tablespoons mustard oil
1 teaspoon cumin seed
1 chopped onion
1 chopped tomato
1 teaspoon ginger paste
1 teaspoon garlic paste
1 teaspoon coriander powder
1 teaspoon red chilli powder
1 teaspoon turmeric powder
Salt to taste
1 ½ cups water
1 teaspoon garam masala
¼ cup chopped coriander leaves

Method

- Soak split skinless chickpeas in water for 1 hour. Drain away water and set aside.
- Peel the potatoes and cut into 4 pieces each.
- Preheat oil in a medium pressure cooker over high heat. Add cumin seeds.
- Add onion and fry till golden brown. Add potatoes, split skinless chickpeas, tomato, ginger paste and garlic paste and fry for 3 minutes.
- Add coriander powder, red chilli powder, turmeric powder and salt. Fry for 10 minutes.
- Add water and garam masala and close the lid of the pressure cooker. Cook till 2 whistles. Garnish with coriander leaves.

Nutritive value per serving

ENERGY	FAT	CHO	C.H	FIBRE	PROTEIN	CALCIUM	IRON	VIT C
Kcal	Gm	Mg	Gm	Gm	Gm	Mg	Mg	Mg
339	11	0	47	15	15	76	5	32

34. Aloo Kachalu

Number of servings: 4

Ingredients

Lemon sized tamarind
¼ cup water
1 ½ tablespoons cumin seeds
4 boiled potatoes
Salt to taste
½ teaspoon rock salt
½ teaspoon red chilli powder

Method

- Soak tamarind in water for ½ an hour. Remove seeds and strain.
- Roast cumin seeds on hot griddle for a minute. Grind into powder
- Peel the potatoes and cut into 5 roundels each. Cut each roundel from the middle to give the shape of semicircle.
- Add tamarind, cumin powder, salt, rock salt and red chilli powder. Eat with small forks or tooth pricks.

Nutritive value per serving

ENERGY	FAT	CHO	C.H	FIBRE	PROTEIN	CALCIUM	IRON	VIT C
Kcal	Gm	Mg	Gm	Gm	Gm	Mg	Mg	Mg
124	1	0	28	3	3	37	3	25

35. Aloo Kulcha

Number of servings: 12

Ingredients

2½ cups refined flour
1 cup semolina
A pinch of soda bi carbonate
4 tablespoons peanut oil
¼ tablespoon baking powder
water
3 boiled potatoes
Salt to taste
1/3 teaspoon red chilli powder

Method

- Transfer refined flour, semolina, soda bi carbonate, peanut oil and baking powder to a large bowl.
- Mix well and knead into a soft dough using water. Set aside for half an hour.
- Peel and grate the potatoes. Add salt and red chilli powder.
- Divide the dough into 6 equal portions. Make balls.
- Flatten the balls. Place equal portions of the potato filling in between and seal the edges properly. Dust with a little flour.
- Roll into 6-7 inches diameter discs. Place them one by one into preheated oven and cook for 3-4 minutes.
- Cut into 2 halves and serve hot with any Indian curry.

Nutritive value per serving

ENERGY	FAT	CHO	C.H	FIBRE	PROTEIN	CALCIUM	IRON	VIT C
Kcal	Gm	Mg	Gm	Gm	Gm	Mg	Mg	Mg
241	7	1	39	2	5	38	2	3

To make kulchas tastier grease them with butter before eating.

36. Potatoes stuffed in puris

Number of servings: 8

Ingredients

4 medium sized potatoes
1 cup peanut oil
1 chopped onion
2 chopped green chillies
Salt to taste
1 teaspoon white pepper
½ cup chopped coriander leaves
2 cups wheat flour
water

Method

- Peel and mash the potatoes
- Preheat 2 tablespoons oil in a small frying pan over high heat. Add onion and green chillies and fry till golden brown.
- Add mashed potatoes, salt and pepper. Fry for 5 minutes. Add coriander leaves. Transfer to a plate.
- Knead wheat flour with water. Divide into 8 equal portions.
- Dust the balls with a little flour. Flatten 1 ball between the palms to form a 2 inches diameter round disc.
- Place 1/8 portion of the potato filling in the middle, enfold and properly seal the edges.
- Dust with flour and flatten with the rolling pin into 5-6 inches diameter disc. Repeat process for the remaining flour and potato filling.
- Preheat the remaining oil in the frying pan over high heat. Fry the discs, one by one over medium heat till they turn pale brown on both the sides. Drain excess oil on absorbent paper. Serve hot.

Nutritive value per serving

ENERGY	FAT	CHO	C.H	FIBRE	PROTEIN	CALCIUM	IRON	VIT C
Kcal	Gm	Mg	Gm	Gm	Gm	Mg	Mg	Mg
273	14	0	33	5	6	42	2	47

Note – approximately, only ½ cup peanut oil will get used.

37. Aloo Litti

Number of servings: 8

Ingredients

4 medium sized potatoes
2 tablespoons peanut oil
1 chopped onion
2 chopped green chillies
8 minced garlic cloves
Salt to taste
1 teaspoon white pepper
½ cup chopped coriander leaves
2½ cups wheat flour
water

Method

- Peel and mash the potatoes
- Preheat 2 tablespoons oil in a small frying pan over high heat. Add onion, green chillies and garlic and fry till golden brown.
- Add mashed potatoes, salt and pepper. Fry for 5 minutes. Add coriander leaves. Transfer to a plate.
- Knead flour with water. Divide into 8 equal portions.
- Dust the balls with a little flour. Flatten one of them between palms into 2 inches diameter round discs.
- Place 1/8 portion of the potato filling in the middle, enfold and properly seal the edges. Give the shape of a ball. Repeat process for the remaining flour and potato filling.
- Place all of them on a preheated oven at 375 degrees F for 10-12 minutes or till the balls get light brown on all the sides. Serve hot.

Nutritive value per serving

ENERGY	FAT	CHO	C.H	FIBRE	PROTEIN	CALCIUM	IRON	VIT C
Kcal	Gm	Mg	Gm	Gm	Gm	Mg	Mg	Mg
225	4	0	42	6	7	51	3	51

To make littis tastier, grease them with ghee before eating.

38. *Potato Roll*

Number of servings: 6

Ingredients

2¾ cups refined flour
A pinch of soda bi carbonate
11 tablespoons peanut oil
Salt to taste
water
6 Medium sized boiled potatoes
2 chopped onions
4 chopped green chillies
1 lemon
6 tablespoons tomato sauce

Method

- Add soda bi carbonate, 2 tablespoons refined oil and salt to refined flour. Knead with water.
- Peel the potatoes, mash and add salt.
- Divide the flour into 6 equal portions. Make balls.
- Dust the balls with flour and roll each ball into 8-10 diameters round discs.
- Preheat a griddle over high heat. Cook the discs on both the sides, applying 1 ½ tablespoons oil. Remove from fire.
- Put 1/6 portion of the mashed potatoes in the middle of each disc. Spread chopped onion and green chillies over the potatoes.
- Add a little lemon juice and sprinkle 1 tablespoon tomato sauce over each disc. Give the shape of a roll. Seal ½ of the roll with a paper so that the filling does not fall down while eating. Serve hot.

Nutritive value per serving

ENERGY	FAT	CHO	C.H	FIBRE	PROTEIN	CALCIUM	IRON	VIT C
Kcal	Gm	Mg	Gm	Gm	Gm	Mg	Mg	Mg
467	25	0	55	4	7	30	3	97

39. Potato Fritters

Number of servings: 8

Ingredients

2 medium sized potatoes
1 tablespoons grated ginger
2 tablespoons chopped onion
1 chopped green chilli
1 egg
Salt to taste
½ teaspoon white pepper
½ cup peanut oil

Method

- Peel and grate potatoes. Add ginger, onion and chilli.
- Beat the egg. Add to the potatoes. Add salt and white pepper.
- Preheat oil in a small frying pan over high heat. Fry spoonfuls of the potato and egg mixture for 3-4 minutes. Drain on absorbent paper. Serve hot.

Nutritive value per serving

ENERGY	FAT	CHO	C.H	FIBRE	PROTEIN	CALCIUM	IRON	VIT C
Kcal	Gm	Mg	Gm	Gm	Gm	Mg	Mg	Mg
118	10	23	7	1	2	8	trace	20

Note – approximately, only 1/3 cup peanut oil will get used.

40. Potato Chilli

Number of servings: 4

Ingredients

2 large sized potatoes
2 small onions
1 capsicum
4 green chillies
6 Tablespoons corn flour
2 cups water
½ teaspoon ajinomoto
Salt to taste
1 teaspoon white pepper
½ cup peanut oil
1 tablespoon garlic paste
1 tablespoon grated ginger
1 teaspoon chilli sauce
½ teaspoon vinegar
½ tablespoon Soya sauce

Method

- Peel and cut potatoes into 3 roundels lengthwise. Cut each roundel lengthwise into 4 pieces. Cut onion and capsicum into squares. Slit the green chillies.
- Add a little water to the corn flour and make a batter of medium consistency. Add a pinch of ajinomoto, salt and ½ teaspoon pepper. Dip the potato pieces into this paste.
- Preheat oil in a medium frying pan over high heat. Deep-fry the potatoes till they turn golden brown. Transfer to a plate. Drain away excess oil on an absorbent paper.
- Remove extra oil leaving only 1 tablespoon oil in the frying pan. Add garlic and ginger paste. After a minute add the vegetables. Sauté for 3 minutes.
- Add chilli sauce, Soya sauce, vinegar, ajinomoto, salt and water.
- Bring to a boil. Add potato and the left over corn flour batter. When the gravy thickens remove from fire. Serve immediately. Add more water if a thinner gravy is desired.

Nutritive value per serving

ENERGY	FAT	CHO	C.H	FIBRE	PROTEIN	CALCIUM	IRON	VIT C
Kcal	Gm	Mg	Gm	Gm	Gm	Mg	Mg	Mg
267	14	0	33	4	4	37	2	153

Note – approximately only 1/3 cup peanut oil will get used.

41. *Potato Tehri*

Number of servings: 2

Ingredients

2 potatoes
1 onion
2 green chillies
2 ½ tablespoons peanut oil
1 tablespoon cumin seeds
2 black cardamoms
2 bay leaves
2 cups rice
Salt to taste
½ teaspoon turmeric powder
4 cups water
1 teaspoon garam masala

Method

- Peel and cut potatoes into 4 pieces each. Chop onion into very thin roundels and slit green chillies.
- Preheat oil in a medium pressure cooker over high heat. Add cumin seeds, black cardamoms and bay leaves.
- After half a minute add onion and fry till golden brown. Add potatoes and green chillies
- After 2 minutes add rice, salt and turmeric powder. Fry over medium heat for 5 minutes.
- Add water and garam masala and cook over high heat till 1 whistle.

Nutritive value per serving

ENERGY	FAT	CHO	CH	FIBRE	PROTEIN	CALCIUM	IRON	VIT C
Kcal	Gm	Mg	Gm	Gm	Gm	Mg	Mg	Mg
995	20	0	135	8	19	146	13	138

42. Aloo Paneer

Number of servings: 6

Ingredients

4 medium sized boiled potatoes
150 grams cottage cheese paneer
4 tablespoons peanut oil
4 green cardamoms
2 sticks cinnamon
1 finely chopped onion
2 chopped green chillies
Salt to taste
1 teaspoon coriander powder
½ teaspoon red chilli powder
1 finely chopped tomato
½ cup water
1 teaspoon garam masala
½ cup chopped coriander leaves

Method

- Peel and cut potatoes into 6 pieces each. Cut cottage cheese into cubes
- Preheat oil in a medium frying pan over high heat. Add cardamoms and cinnamon. Add cottage cheese and fry till they turn brown. Transfer to a plate.
- In the remaining oil add onion and fry till golden brown. Add potato and green chillies and fry for 3 minutes.
- Add salt, coriander powder, red chilli powder and tomato. Fry till fat leaves the sides. Add cottage cheese and fry for another 5 minutes.
- Add water and garam masala. Cover and bring to a boil. Remove from fire. Garnish with coriander leaves.

Nutritive value per serving

ENERGY	FAT	CHO	C.H	FIBRE	PROTEIN	CALCIUM	IRON	VIT C
Kcal	Gm	Mg	Gm	Gm	Gm	Mg	Mg	Mg
210	10	2	25	5	7	105	4	73

43. Aloo Ambat

Number of servings: 3

Ingredients

1 cup split red grams
3 medium sized potatoes
1 teaspoon garlic paste
Salt to taste
1 teaspoon turmeric powder
2 cups water
1 ½ tablespoons ghee
1 teaspoon black mustard seeds
1 small onion, finely chopped.
1 small tomato finely chopped
1 chopped green chilli

Method

- Wash and transfer split red grams to a pressure cooker.
- Peel the potatoes and cut into 2 pieces each. Add to the split red grams.
- Add garlic paste, salt, turmeric powder and water and cook over high heat till 1 whistle over high heat. Remove from fire. Add a little hot water if required.
- Preheat ghee in a small frying pan. Add black mustard seeds. After half a minute add onion and fry till golden brown.
- Add tomato and green chilli and fry till the tomatoes get mashed. Add to the cooked split red grams and potatoes.

Nutritive value per serving

ENERGY	FAT	CHO	C.H	FIBRE	PROTEIN	CALCIUM	IRON	VIT C
Kcal	Gm	Mg	Gm	Gm	Gm	Mg	Mg	Mg
418	8	17	69	20	20	70	5	72

44. Stuffed Tikkis

Number of servings: 8

Ingredients

6 large boiled potatoes
½ cup chopped coriander leaves
Salt to taste
1½ teaspoon white pepper
1 small carrot
4 tablespoons cheese
2½ tablespoons peanut oil

Method

- Peel the potatoes and grate.
- Add coriander leaves, salt and white pepper. Mix well.
- Divide into 8 equal portions. Make balls and then press gently between the palms.
- Grate the carrot. Divide into 4 equal portions. Spread each portion over 4 potato tikkis. Top each with 1 tablespoon cheese and cover with the remaining 4 tikkis. Press gently.
- Preheat a non-stick griddle over high heat. Place the potato tikkis on it.
- Drizzle 1 tablespoon oil at the sides of the potato tikkis. Cook till one side of the potatoes get reddish brown.
- Turn them carefully to the other side. Drizzle remaining oil and cook till other side turns brown. Serve piping hot.

Nutritive value per serving

ENERGY	FAT	CHO	C.H	FIBRE	PROTEIN	CALCIUM	IRON	VIT C
Kcal	Gm	Mg	Gm	Gm	Gm	Mg	Mg	Mg
214	11	3	28	4	3	67	1	21

45. *Potato Sago*

Number of servings: 6

Ingredients

4 boiled medium sized potatoes
Salt to taste
1 tablespoon white pepper
½ cup sago (sabudana)
¾ cup peanut oil

Method

- Peel and grate the potatoes. Add salt and pepper.
- Soak sago in water for 10 minutes. Drain away water and mix sago with potatoes.
- Divide into 6 equal portions. Make balls and pres between palms.
- Preheat oil over medium heat and fry the potatoes over medium heat till they turn brown. Serve hot

Nutritive value per serving

ENERGY	FAT	CHO	C.H	FIBRE	PROTEIN	CALCIUM	IRON	VIT C
Kcal	Gm	Mg	Gm	Gm	Gm	Mg	Mg	Mg
292	19	3	29	4	5	43	1	9

Note – approximately only 1/3 cup peanut oil will get used.

46. Aloo Dum

Number of servings: 4

Ingredients

4 large sized potatoes
1 onion
2 tomatoes
6 garlic cloves
¼ cup mustard oil
1 teaspoon cumin seeds
2 black cardamoms
2 bay leaves
2 red chillies
2 sticks cinnamon
2 tablespoons grated ginger
1 teaspoon turmeric powder
1 tablespoon coriander powder
½ teaspoon red chilli powder
Salt to taste
1½ cups water
1½ teaspoon garam masala
½ cup chopped coriander leaves

Method

- Peel and cut potatoes into 2 pieces each.
- Chop onion, tomatoes, garlic and grind into a smooth paste using a little water.
- Preheat oil in a medium pressure cooker. Fry the potatoes over medium heat till they turn golden brown.
- Transfer the potatoes to a plate.
- In the remaining oil add cumin seeds, cardamom, bay leaves, red chillies and cinnamon.
- After a minute, add the ground paste, ginger, turmeric powder, coriander powder and red chilli powder and fry till fat starts leaving the sides.
- Add fried potatoes and salt. Fry over medium heat for 3 minutes. Add water and close the lid of the pressure cooker. Cook till 1 whistle. Garnish with coriander leaves.

Nutritive value per serving

ENERGY	FAT	CHO	C.H	FIBRE	PROTEIN	CALCIUM	IRON	VIT C
Kcal	Gm	Mg	Gm	Gm	Gm	Mg	Mg	Mg
304	15	0	41	8	6	144	6	134

47. Aloo Khichri

Number of servings: 2

Ingredients

8 smallest size potatoes
1 onion
3 tablespoons mustard oil
1 teaspoon cumin seeds
2 red chillies
1 bay leaf
4 green cardamoms
4 cloves
1 teaspoon garlic paste
1 teaspoon ginger paste
½ cup shelled green peas
½ cup rice
½ cup split red grams
½ teaspoon turmeric powder
Salt to taste
2¾ cups water

Method

- Peel the potatoes, chop the onion.
- Preheat mustard oil over high heat in a medium frying pan. Add cumin seeds, red chillies, bay leaf, cardamoms and cloves.
- After a minute add onion and fry till golden brown. Add potatoes, garlic paste and ginger paste. Fry over medium heat for 5 minutes.
- Add green peas and fry for another 2 minutes. Remove from fire.
- Wash rice and split red grams. Transfer to a medium pressure cooker. Add turmeric powder, salt and fried vegetables.
- Add water and cook over high heat till 1 whistle.

Nutritive value per serving

ENERGY	FAT	CHO	C.H	FIBRE	PROTEIN	CALCIUM	IRON	VIT C
Kcal	Gm	Mg	Gm	Gm	Gm	Mg	Mg	Mg
778	26	0	122	27	24	230	10	202

If small potatoes are not available in the market then use medium sized potatoes and cut into 2 or 4 pieces according to their size.

48. Potato Bonda

Number of servings: 8

Ingredients

6 boiled potatoes
1 cup peanut oil
2 teaspoons mustard seeds
1 sprig curry leaves
1 finely chopped onion
2 green chillies
1½ tablespoons grated ginger
1 teaspoons turmeric powder
Salt to taste
½ lemon
1½ cups gram flour
A pinch of soda bi carbonate
water

Method

- Peel the potatoes and mash.
- Preheat 2 tablespoons oil in a small frying pan. Add mustard seeds and curry leaves.
- After a minute add onion, green chillies and grated ginger and fry for 3 minutes.
- Add potatoes, turmeric powder, salt and lime juice. Fry for 2 minutes. Remove from fire.
- Prepare a thick batter using gram flour, salt, soda bi carbonate and a little water.
- Divide the potatoes into 8 equal portions. Make balls.
- Preheat remaining oil over high heat. Dip the balls in the batter and deep fry 3-4 at a time till they turn pale brown.

Nutritive value per serving

ENERGY	FAT	CHO	C.H	FIBRE	PROTEIN	CALCIUM	IRON	VIT C
Kcal	Gm	Mg	Gm	Gm	Gm	Mg	Mg	Mg
336	19	0	38	3	5	23	2	48

Note – approximately, only 2/3 cup peanut oil will get used.

49. Pav Bhaji

Number of servings: 4

Ingredients

4 boiled potatoes
2 tablespoons split moong beans
3 tablespoons peanut oil
1 chopped onion
6 garlic cloves, slit
3 chopped tomatoes
Salt to taste
1 teaspoon red chilli powder
½ teaspoon turmeric powder
2 tablespoons pav bhaji masala
1½ cups water
3 tablespoons butter
½ lemon
4 pavs
½ cup chopped coriander leaves

Method

- Peel and mash the potatoes. Soak split mung beans in a little water for 30 minutes.
- Preheat oil in a medium frying pan over high heat. Add onion and garlic and fry till golden brown. Add split mung beans, tomato and salt and cook till tomatoes get mashed.
- Add potatoes, red chilli powder, turmeric powder and pav bhaji masala. Fry for 5 minutes.
- Add water and bring to a boil. Add 1 tablespoon butter and lemon juice. Remove from fire.
- Slit the pavs in between. Preheat a griddle over high heat. Lightly, roast the pavs. Add butter. Remove from fire.
- Serve hot bhaji and pav. Garnish bhaji with coriander leaves.

Nutritive value per serving

ENERGY	FAT	CHC	C.H	FIBRE	PROTEIN	CALCIUM	IRON	VIT C
Kcal	Gm	Mg	Gm	Gm	Gm	Mg	Mg	Mg
413	21	24	51	7	9	131	5	70

50. *Potato Patties*

Number of servings: 8

Ingredients

6 large boiled potatoes
3 slices of bread
½ lemon
Salt to taste
1 cup peanut oil
1 ½ teaspoons coriander seeds
1 cup grated coconut
2 minced green chillies
4 tablespoons chopped coriander leaves
½ cup refined flour
water

Method

- Peel and mash potatoes. Soak breads in a bowl of water for a few seconds. Press gently between palms to drain away water.
- Mix with potatoes. Add salt and lemon juice. Divide into 8 equal portions.
- Preheat 1 ½ tablespoons oil in a small frying pan. Add coriander seeds.
- After a minute add coconut, green chillies and coriander leaves. Fry over medium heat for 3-4 minutes. Remove from fire.
- Shape potatoes into cups and stuff with equal portions of fried coconut. Close the edges and give round shapes.
- Make a batter of medium consistency using refined flour and water. Add a little salt.
- Preheat oil in a small frying pan. Dip potato balls in the batter and deep fry till brown.

Nutritive value per serving

ENERGY	FAT	CHO	C.H	FIBRE	PROTEIN	CALCIUM	IRON	VIT C
Kcal	Gm	Mg	Gm	Gm	Gm	Mg	Mg	Mg
352	23	trace	35	3	4	36	2	52

Note – approximately, only 2/3 cup peanut oil will get used.

51. Cashew Potato Curry

Number of servings: 4

Ingredients

- 8 medium sized boiled potatoes
- ¾ cup cashew nuts
- 2 chopped onions
- 2 tablespoons chopped ginger
- 3 tablespoons peanut oil
- 2 black cardamoms
- 2 pieces of cinnamon stick.
- 1 teaspoon red chilli powder
- ½ cup grated coconut
- Salt to taste
- 1 cup water
- 2 teaspoons garam masala

Method

- Peel and cut each potato into 2 pieces.
- Soak the cashew nuts in hot water for 20 minutes. Drain water and grind cashew nuts into a paste
- Grind together onion and ginger.
- Preheat oil in a big frying pan. Add cardamoms and cinnamon sticks.
- Add onion paste and fry till golden brown.
- Add potatoes and cashew paste. Fry for 3 minutes. Add red chilli powder and grated coconut, Fry for another 3-4 minutes. Add salt and water.
- Cook till water almost dries up. Add garam masala. Remove from fire.

Nutritive value per serving

ENERGY	FAT	CHO	C.H	FIBRE	PROTEIN	CALCIUM	IRON	VIT C
Kcal	Gm	Mg	Gm	Gm	Gm	Mg	Mg	Mg
463	26	0	54	10	10	99	5	42

52. Potato Cashew Fry

Number of servings: 4

Ingredients

1 cup cashew nuts
2 boiled potatoes
2 tablespoons peanut oil
1 onion cut into thin roundels
1 slit green chilli
1 teaspoon ginger paste
1 teaspoon garlic paste
Salt to taste
1 teaspoon white pepper
¼ lemon
¼ cup chopped coriander leaves

Method

- Soak cashew nuts in hot water for 10 minutes.
- Peel and cut potatoes into cubes.
- Preheat oil in a medium frying pan over high heat.
- Add onion and green chilli and fry for 3 minutes. Add ginger and garlic paste and fry for another 3 minutes.
- Add potatoes, cashew nuts, salt and pepper. Fry over high heat for 5 minutes.
- Add lemon juice. Remove from fire. Garnish with coriander leaves.

Nutritive value per serving

ENERGY	FAT	CHO	C.H	FIBRE	PROTEIN	CALCIUM	IRON	VIT C
Kcal	Gm	Mg	Gm	Gm	Gm	Mg	Mg	Mg
320	23	0	26	4	8	52	3	54

53. *Potato Toast*

Number of servings: 4

Ingredients

2 boiled potatoes
1 small, finely chopped onion
2 finely chopped green chilli
¼ cup chopped coriander leaves
Salt to taste
2 boiled eggs
½ teaspoon pepper
4 bread slices
⅔ cup peanut oil

Method

- Peel and mash the potatoes.
- Add onion, green chillies, coriander leaves and salt.
- Beat the eggs properly. Add salt and pepper.
- Cut each bread slice into 2 rectangular pieces.
- Stuff equal portions of potatoes in between.
- Preheat oil in a small frying pan over high heat.
- Dip each stuffed bread into the egg batter and deep fry one at a time till the potato toast is crisp and brown.

Nutritive value per serving

ENERGY	FAT	CHO	C H	FIBRE	PROTEIN	CALCIUM	IRON	VIT C
Kcal	Gm	Mg	Gm	Gm	Gm	Mg	Mg	Mg
475	35	96	36	4	8	98	3	73

Note – approximately only ½ cup peanut oil will get used.

54. *Potatoes with Coconut*

Number of servings: 4

Ingredients

4 boiled medium sized potatoes
1 tablespoon peanut oil
1 teaspoon urad lentil
1 teaspoon black mustard seeds
1 sprig curry leaves
1 chopped onion
2 chopped green chillies
1 cup grated coconut
½ lemon
Salt to taste

Method

- Peel and cut potatoes into cubes.
- Preheat oil in a small frying pan over high heat. Add urad lentil, black mustard seeds and curry leaves.
- Add the potatoes, onion, green chillies, coconut, lemon juice and salt. Mix well. Remove from fire.

Nutritive value per serving

ENERGY	FAT	CHO	C.H	FIBRE	PROTEIN	CALCIUM	IRON	VIT C
Kcal	Gm	Mg	Gm	Gm	Gm	Mg	Mg	Mg
271	12	0	39	4	5	29	2	84

55. Aloo Puri

Number of servings: 10

Ingredients

3 medium sized boiled potatoes
2 cups wheat flour
Salt to taste
1 teaspoon red chilli powder
1 cup water
1¼ cups peanut oil

Method

- Peel and mash the potatoes.
- To the wheat flour, add mashed potatoes, salt and red chilli powder.
- Knead into a stiff dough with water. Divide into 10 equal portions. Make balls. Gently press the balls between the palms.
- Dust with a little flour and roll each ball into 3-4 inches diameter discs.
- Preheat oil over high heat in a medium frying pan.
- Deep-fry the discs one at a time over medium heat till they turn brown on both the sides.

Nutritive value per serving

ENERGY	FAT	CHO	CH	FIBRE	PROTEIN	CALCIUM	IRON	VIT C
Kcal	Gm	Mg	Gm	Gm	Gm	Mg	Mg	Mg
254	17	0	24	4	4	12	1	7

Note – approximately, only ½ cup peanut oil will get used.

56. Samosa

Number of servings: 12

Ingredients

1½ cups peanut oil
Salt to taste
A pinch of soda bi carbonate
2 cups refined flour
¾ cup water
6 medium sized boiled potatoes
1/3 cup peanuts
1 chopped onion
2 chopped green chillies
½ teaspoon turmeric powder
½ teaspoon garam masala powder

Method

- Add 4 tablespoons peanut oil, a pinch of salt and soda bi carbonate to refined floor. Knead into a smooth dough using water.
- Divide the dough into 12 equal portions. Make balls and flatten between palms.
- Peel and mash the potatoes.
- Preheat 4 tablespoons oil in a small frying pan over high heat. Add peanuts and fry for 3 minutes. Set aside.
- In the remaining oil add onions and green chillies and fry till golden brown.
- Add mashed potatoes, green chillies, salt, turmeric powder and garam masala. Fry for 5 minutes. Remove from fire. Add fried peanuts.

- Roll the flour balls into 4 inches diameter discs. With a knife, cut in the center to form 2 semicircles of 1 disc.
- Make a cone of each semicircle. Stuff the prepared potato filling in equal quantities.
- Seal the edges using 1-2 drops of water.
- Preheat oil in the frying pan. Deep fry 4 at a time till they turn brown. Serve hot with tomato sauce.

Nutritive value per serving

ENERGY	FAT	CHO	C.H	FIBRE	PROTEIN	CALCIUM	IRON	VIT C
Kcal	Gm	Mg	Gm	Gm	Gm	Mg	Mg	Mg
376	25	2	36	3	5	38	2	25

Note – approximately, only 1 cup peanut oil will get used.

57. Potato Snackies

Number of servings: 8

Ingredients

6 boiled potatoes
1 cup boiled green peas
1 spring onion
¼ cup refined flour
1½ tablespoons melted butter
Salt to taste
Pepper to taste

Method

- Peel and mash the potatoes. Mash the green peas. Finely chop the spring onion.
- Mix all the ingredients together. Roll into 1-inch thick cylinders.
- Cut into 8 equal portions.
- Transfer to a greased baking tray or baking sheet and bake in a hot oven till the potatoes turn golden brown and crisp.

Nutritive value per serving

ENERGY	FAT	CHO	C.H	FIBRE	PROTEIN	CALCIUM	IRON	VIT C
Kcal	Gm	Mg	Gm	Gm	Gm	Mg	Mg	Mg
216	9	9	32	4	4	48	1	17

58. Stuffed Capsicums

Number of servings: 4

Ingredients

4 large capsicums
4 medium sized boiled potatoes
1 onion
2 tablespoons peanut oil
Salt to taste
Pepper to taste
¼ lemon
½ cup chopped coriander leaves
4 tablespoons cheese

Method

- Slice the tops of capsicum. Remove seeds and apply salt inside. Keep upside down for at least 10 minutes.
- Peel and mash the potatoes. Finely chop onion.
- Preheat oil in a small frying pan. Add onion and fry till golden brown.
- Add potatoes, salt and pepper. Fry over high heat for 10 minutes.
- Add lemon juice and coriander leaves. Mix well.
- Stuff capsicums with equal portions of potato stuffing. Top with equal portions of cheese.
- Cook in a slow oven till capsicums are tender. Serve hot.

Nutritive value per serving

ENERGY	FAT	CHO	C H	FIBRE	PROTEIN	CALCIUM	IRON	VIT C
Kcal	Gm	Mg	Gm	Gm	Gm	Mg	Mg	Mg
209	7	0	34	5	5	71	3	154

59. Potato Kofta

Number of servings: 6

Ingredients

4 large sized boiled potatoes
Salt to taste
½ tablespoon white pepper
1 chopped green chilli
1 finely chopped onion
1 cup chopped coriander leaves
1 cup gram flour
2¾ cups water
½ cup peanut oil
2 red chillies
1 bay leaf
½ cup onion paste
1 tablespoon ginger paste
1 tablespoon garlic paste
2 chopped tomatoes
½ teaspoon turmeric powder

Method

- Peel and mash potatoes, add salt, white pepper, green chillies, onion and ½ cup coriander leaves. Divide into 6 equal portions. Make balls. Press gently in between.
- Make a medium consistency paste of gram flour using water. Add a little salt.
- Preheat oil over high heat in a medium frying pan. Dip the potato balls and deep fry till golden brown.
- Remove excess oil, if more than 3 tablespoons oil is left in the frying pan.
- Add red chillies and bay leaf. Add onion paste, ginger paste, garlic paste and fry over high heat for 3 minutes. Add tomatoes, turmeric powder and salt and fry till tomatoes are mashed. Add remaining water, cover and bring to a boil.
- Add fried potatoes and cook for 2 minutes. Garnish with the remaining coriander leaves.

Nutritive value per serving

ENERGY	FAT	CHO	C.H	FIBRE	PROTEIN	CALCIUM	IRON	VIT C
Kcal	Gm	Mg	Gm	Gm	Gm	Mg	Mg	Mg
259	10	0	39	4	5	30	2	93

Note – approximately, only 1/4 cup peanut oil will get used.

60. Masala Dosa

Number of servings: 4

Ingredients

- 5 boiled potatoes
- 1/3 cup peanut oil
- 1/3 cup peanuts
- 1 1/2 teaspoons black mustard seeds
- 1 sprig curry leaves
- 1 chopped onion
- 2 chopped green chillies
- 1 teaspoon turmeric powder
- Salt to taste
- 1 cup semolina
- 2 teaspoons refined flour
- 1/2 cup buttermilk.

Method

- Peel and mash the potatoes.
- Preheat 3 tablespoons oil in a medium frying pan over medium heat.
- Add peanuts and fry till 3 minutes. Transfer to a bowl.
- In the remaining oil add black mustard seeds and curry leaves. After half a minute add onion and green chillies and fry till golden brown.
- Add potatoes, turmeric powder and salt and fry over high heat for 5 minutes. Add peanuts. Mix well. Remove from fire.
- Mix together, semolina, refined flour, buttermilk and a little salt. Set aside for at least half an hour.
- Preheat griddle over high heat. Smear the griddle with a half cut onion.
- Pour 1/4 of the batter with a ladle and move round and round to form a 8 inches diameter disc. Put a little fat around it and turn over.
- Put 1/4 potato stuffing on one side of the disc. Fold the disc to give the shape of a semi circle. Repeat process for the remaining batter and potatoes. Serve hot.

Nutritive value per serving

ENERGY	FAT	CHO	C.H	FIBRE	PROTEIN	CALCIUM	IRON	VIT C
Kcal	Gm	Mg	Gm	Gm	Gm	Mg	Mg	Mg
539	25	1	67	6	14	77	4	87

61. *Aloo Ka Salan*

Number of servings: 4

Ingredients

- 4 medium potatoes
- 3 tablespoons ghee
- 4 green cardamoms
- 2 cloves
- 1 cinnamon stick
- 2 teaspoon ginger paste
- 2 teaspoons garlic paste
- 2/3 cup onion paste
- 2 teaspoons coriander powder
- 1 teaspoon red chilli powder
- 1/2 teaspoon turmeric powder
- 2 cups water
- 1/2 cup whipped yogurt
- Salt to taste
- 1/2 teaspoon garam masala
- 4 slit green chillies
- 1 finely chopped tomato
- 1 tablespoon lemon juice

Method

- Cut each potato with skin lengthwise, into 8 pieces. Boil till they get tender.
- Heat ghee in a medium frying pan over medium heat. Add green cardamoms, cloves and cinnamon stick and stir till green cardamoms begin to change color.
- Add ginger and garlic paste and stir for 2 minutes. Add onion paste and fry for 3-4 minutes.
- Add coriander powder, red chilli powder and turmeric powder dissolved in 3 tablespoons water. Stir-fry till moisture evaporates.
- Remove frying pan from fire. Stir in yogurt and return frying pan to fire and fry till the fat leaves the sides.
- Add water and bring to a boil over high heat. Reduce to medium heat, and add potatoes and salt. Bring to a boil.
- Simmer and stir for 5 minutes. Add garam masala and remove from fire.
- Garnish with green chillies and tomato. Add lemon juice.

Nutritive value per serving

ENERGY	FAT	CHO	C.H	FIBRE	PROTEIN	CALCIUM	IRON	VIT C
Kcal	Gm	Mg	Gm	Gm	Gm	Mg	Mg	Mg
287	13	30	42	9	6	157	5	149

62. Sweet Parathas

Number of servings: 12

Ingredients

½ cup warm milk

½ cup sugar

2 boiled potatoes

A pinch of eating soda

1 tablespoon green cardamom powder

2½ cups wheat flour

½ cup ghee

Method

- Mix together milk and sugar and let the sugar completely dissolve in milk.
- Peel and mash the potatoes.
- Add milk and potato to wheat flour along with eating soda, green cardamom powder and 1½ tablespoons ghee and knead into smooth dough.
- Divide the dough into 12 equal portions. Make balls, and roll into 4 cm diameter discs with a rolling pin. Use a little wheat flour to dust the discs while rolling.
- Cook each disc on a preheated griddle over high heat till they turn brown on both the sides. Apply ghee while cooking each disc.

Nutritive value per serving

ENERGY	FAT	CHO	C.H	FIBRE	PROTEIN	CALCIUM	IRON	VIT C
Kcal	Gm	Mg	Gm	Gm	Gm	Mg	Mg	Mg
220	10	25	31	4	4	25	1	4

63. *Potato Halwa*

Number of servings: 4

Ingredients

4 boiled potatoes
¼ cup milk
½ cup sugar
1 teaspoon green cardamom powder
½ cup khoya
2 teaspoons ghee
4 chopped pistachios.

Method

- Peel and mash potatoes.
- Mix together milk and sugar and let the sugar get dissolved in milk completely.
- Preheat the milk in a medium frying pan over high heat. Add potatoes and cook over medium heat for 3 minutes
- Add green cardamom powder, khoya and ghee and fry till the milk dries up.
- Garnish with pistachios and serve.

Nutritive value per serving

ENERGY	FAT	CHO	C.H	FIBRE	PROTEIN	CALCIUM	IRON	VIT C
Kcal	Gm	Mg	Gm	Gm	Gm	Mg	Mg	Mg
369	8	25	70	2	7	175	1	26

64. Masala Muri

Number of servings: 4

Ingredients

Lemon sized tamarind
¼ cup water
2 tablespoons sugar
¼ teaspoon red chilli powder
2 boiled potato
4 cups puffed rice
1 chopped green chilli
¼ cup chopped coriander leaves
Salt to taste
⅓ cup finely chopped coconut

Method

- Soak tamarind in water for 20 minutes. Strain the juice.
- Add sugar and let it dissolve. Add red chilli powder. Mix well.
- Peel and finely chop potatoes.
- Add tamarind juice and potatoes to the puffed rice. Add the remaining ingredients and mix well. Serve immediately.

Nutritive value per serving

ENERGY	FAT	CHO	C.H	FIBRE	PROTEIN	CALCIUM	IRON	VIT C
Kcal	Gm	Mg	Gm	Gm	Gm	Mg	Mg	Mg
178	3	0	38	3	3	37	2	50

65. Peanuts and Potato

Number of servings: 4

Ingredients

2 large sized potatoes
2 chopped green chillies
1 cup peanut oil
½ cup peanuts
Salt
1 tablespoon lemon juice

Method

- Peel and cut potatoes into 4 roundels each. Finely cut each roundel lengthwise.
- Preheat oil in a small frying pan over high heat.
- Deep-fry the potatoes in 2 batches till they are crisp.
- Transfer to a kitchen paper to remove excess oil.
- In the remaining oil fry peanuts till they turn color. Transfer to the kitchen paper to remove excess oil.
- Mix together fried potatoes, peanuts, green chillies, salt and lemon juice. Serve immediately.

Nutritive value per serving

ENERGY	FAT	CHO	C.H	FIBRE	PROTEIN	CALCIUM	IRON	VIT C
Kcal	Gm	Mg	Gm	Gm	Gm	Mg	Mg	Mg
321	27	0	16	3	6	25	2	68

Note – approximately, only 1/3 cup peanut oil will get used.

66. Baked Cutlets in Gravy

Number of servings: 6

Ingredients

4 large boiled potatoes
1 finely chopped onions
2 chopped green chillies
½ cup chopped coriander leaves
½ lemon
Salt to taste
¾ cup refined flour
water
1 cup bread crumbs
¾ cup peanut oil
3 tomatoes
⅓ teaspoon red chilli powder
2 tablespoons tomato sauce
½ cup grated cheese

Method

- Peel and mash the potatoes.
- Add onion, green chillies, coriander leaves, lemon juice and salt. Divide into 6 equal portions. Give any shape of your choice.
- Make a batter of refined flour and water. Dip the cutlets in the batter and roll into the breadcrumbs.
- Preheat oil in a small frying pan. Deep-fry the cutlets 2 at a time till they turn crisp. Transfer to a kitchen paper to remove excess oil.
- Chop the tomatoes and cook in a small pressure cooker over high heat in 1cup water till 1 whistle.
- After the tomatoes cool down, take out the soup by passing the tomatoes through a sieve.
- Add red chilli powder, tomato sauce and a little salt to the soup and boil for 15 minutes.
- Arrange the cutlets in a baking dish. Pour the tomato gravy over it. Garnish with cheese and bake in a preheated oven at 450 degrees F for 5 minutes. Serve hot.

Nutritive value per serving

ENERGY	FAT	CHO	C.H	FIBRE	PROTEIN	CALCIUM	IRON	VIT C
Kcal	Gm	Mg	Gm	Gm	Gm	Mg	Mg	Mg
334	14	0	48	4	7	92	4	82

67. Potatoes in Sesame Seeds

Number of servings: 4

Ingredients

4 medium sized potatoes
½ cup sesame seeds
1 cup water
⅓ cup mustard oil
½ tablespoons black mustard seeds
2 red chillies
1 sprig curry leaves
1 large onion, chopped
1 tablespoon ginger paste
1 tablespoon garlic paste
½ teaspoon turmeric powder
1 teaspoon red chilli powder
2½ tablespoons tamarind pulp
Salt to taste
1 teaspoon garam masala

Method

- Peel the potatoes and cut each into 3 roundels. Cut each roundel into 3 pieces.
- Preheat a griddle over high heat and roast sesame seeds till they turn light red. Make a smooth paste using ¼ cup water.
- Preheat oil in a heavy bottomed pan. Fry the potatoes lightly in 2 batches over high heat. Transfer to a plate.
- In the remaining oil add black mustard seeds, red chillies and curry leaves. After a minute add onion and fry till golden brown. Add ginger and garlic paste and fry for 2-3 minutes.
- Add turmeric powder and sesame paste and fry till the mixture leaves the fat.
- Add red chilli powder, tamarind pulp, remaining water and salt and bring to a boil.
- Add potatoes and simmer and cover till the potatoes get tender. Add garam masala

Nutritive value per serving

ENERGY	FAT	CHO	C.H	FIBRE	PROTEIN	CALCIUM	IRON	VIT C
Kcal	Gm	Mg	Gm	Gm	Gm	Mg	Mg	Mg
413	28	0	37	6	8	216	5	100

68. Aloo Salad

Number of servings: 4

Ingredients

A bunch of mint sprigs
2 cups yogurt
2 boiled potatoes
1 cup boiled chickpeas
Salt to taste
½ teaspoon chilli powder

Method

- Remove mint leaves from the stems. Grind into a smooth paste.
- Mix the mint paste to the curd.
- Peel and chop potatoes. Transfer to a big bowl.
- Add chickpeas, salt and chilli powder.
- Add yogurt and mix well. Chill before serving.

Nutritive value per serving

ENERGY	FAT	CHO	C.H	FIBRE	PROTEIN	CALCIUM	IRON	VIT C
Kcal	Gm	Mg	Gm	Gm	Gm	Mg	Mg	Mg
192	5	16	28	2	9	174	2	13

69. Potato Pickle

Number of servings: 16

Ingredients

16 smallest size potatoes
Salt to taste
¼ teaspoon red chilli powder
½ teaspoon turmeric powder
1 teaspoon mustard powder
¼ teaspoon ajwain
¼ teaspoon black cumin seeds
1 tablespoon mustard oil

Method

- Boil and peel the potatoes. Mix all the ingredients.
- Leave it out in the sun for 2-4 hours.

Nutritive value per serving

ENERGY	FAT	CHO	C.H	FIBRE	PROTEIN	CALCIUM	IRON	VIT C
Kcal	Gm	Mg	Gm	Gm	Gm	Mg	Mg	Mg
33	1	0	6	1	1	3	trace	6

70. Potato Pancake

Number of servings: 4

Ingredients

4 large boiled potatoes
6 teaspoons butter
1 finely chopped onion
Salt
1 teaspoon pepper
½ cup chopped coriander leaves

Method

- Peel and grate the potatoes.
- Preheat 4 teaspoons butter in a medium, non-stick shallow frying pan or non-stick griddle over high heat. Add onion and fry till golden brown.
- Add potatoes, salt, pepper and coriander leaves. Spread the potatoes evenly on the pan and cook over low heat till the potatoes turn golden brown on the underside.
- During cooking add 1 teaspoon of butter at the sides.
- Turn the potato on the other side gently. Add the remaining butter and cook over low heat till the other side also turns golden brown. Cut into 4 pieces and serve hot.

Nutritive value per serving

ENERGY	FAT	CHO	C.H	FIBRE	PROTEIN	CALCIUM	IRON	VIT C
Kcal	Gm	Mg	Gm	Gm	Gm	Mg	Mg	Mg
169	6	16	27	3	4	63	3	46

71. Stuffed Puris

Number of servings: 10

Ingredients

1 cup semolina
1 ¼ cup peanut oil
½ teaspoon ajwain
Salt to taste
1 cup refined flour
water
1 chopped onion
1 chopped green chilies
½ cup green peas
½ teaspoon turmeric powder
2 large sized boiled potatoes

Method

- Add semolina, 4 tablespoons oil, ajwain and salt to refined flour. Knead into a stiff dough using water.
- Divide the dough into 10 equal portions. Make balls. Dust with a little flour and roll into 3 inches diameter discs.
- Preheat oil in a small frying pan over high heat. Deep fry the puris one by one.
- Leaving 3 tablespoons oil, remove excess oil from the frying pan. Add onion and fry till golden brown.
- Add green chillies, green peas, salt and turmeric. Fry for 3-4 minutes.
- Peel and mash the potatoes and add to the frying pan. Fry till potatoes turn golden brown. Remove from fire.
- Divide potatoes into 10 equal portions. Break the upper crust of each fried disc with a finger.
- Put a portion each of the cooked potatoes on each disc and serve.

Nutritive value per serving

ENERGY	FAT	CHO	C.H	FIBRE	PROTEIN	CALCIUM	IRON	VIT C
Kcal	Gm	Mg	Gm	Gm	Gm	Mg	Mg	Mg
354	24	1	31	3	5	22	2	17

Note – approximately, only 1 cup peanut oil will get used.

72. Stuffed Chila

Number of servings: 6

Ingredients

1 ½ cups gram flour
1 ½ cups water
Salt to taste
½ teaspoon ajwain
1 teaspoon turmeric powder
9 tablespoons peanut oil
1 finely chopped onion
2 green chillies
2 large sized boiled potatoes
¼ cup chopped coriander leaves
6 teaspoons tomato sauce

Method

- Mix together gram flour, water, salt, ajwain and half teaspoon turmeric powder and make a smooth batter.
- Preheat 3 tablespoons oil in a frying pan over high heat.
- Fry onion till golden brown. Add green chillies.
- Peel and mash the potatoes. Add along with salt.
- Fry till light brown. Add chopped coriander leaves. Remove from fire.
- Make 6 pancakes (around 6-8 cm in diameter) of the gram flour batter on a non-stick griddle, using remaining oil.
- Fill a portion of the potatoes, Sprinkle 1 teaspoon tomato sauce. Repeat process for the remaining pancakes and potatoes.
- Roll the pancakes. Cover half of each pancake with paper so that the stuffing does not fall down while eating.

Nutritive value per serving

ENERGY	FAT	CHO	C.H	FIBRE	PROTEIN	CALCIUM	IRON	VIT C
Kcal	Gm	Mg	Gm	Gm	Gm	Mg	Mg	Mg
344	21	0	35	2	5	33	3	53

73. Omelets with Potato Stuffing

Number of servings: 1

Ingredients

2½ tablespoons peanut oil
½ cup finely chopped onion
1 chopped green chilli
1 chopped capsicum
1 medium sized boiled potato
Salt to taste
¼ teaspoon pepper
2 eggs
1 tablespoon tomato sauce.

Method

- Preheat 1½ tablespoons oil in a small frying pan over high heat. Add onion and green chillies and sauté for 3 minutes.
- Add capsicum and sauté for another 3 minutes.
- Peel and mash potato. Add along with salt and pepper. Fry till potatoes turn light brown. Remove from fire.
- Whip the eggs. Add salt and make 2 omelets using the remaining oil.
- Spread the potatoes over one of the omelets. Sprinkle sauce over the potatoes and cover with the other omelet. Serve hot.

Nutritive value per serving

ENERGY	FAT	CHO	C.H	FIBRE	PROTEIN	CALCIUM	IRON	VIT C
Kcal	Gm	Mg	Gm	Gm	Gm	Mg	Mg	Mg
612	43	374	43	7	17	91	4	246

74. Shallow Fried Potatoes

Number of servings: 10

Ingredients

2 medium-sized potatoes

Salt to taste

½ teaspoon turmeric powder

¼ teaspoon red chilli powder

1 teaspoon garlic paste

2 tablespoons mustard oil

Method

- Cut each potato into 5 roundels. (Preferably with the peel on)
- Wash and add salt, turmeric powder, red chilli powder and garlic paste.
- Preheat mustard oil on a griddle or frying pan and shallow fry the potatoes till they get tender. Serve hot.

Nutritive value per serving

ENERGY	FAT	CHO	C.H	FIBRE	PROTEIN	CALCIUM	IRON	VIT C
Kcal	Gm	Mg	Gm	Gm	Gm	Mg	Mg	Mg
44	3	0	5	trace	1	3	trace	5

75. Potato Soup

Number of servings: 1

Ingredients

1 teaspoon butter
1 small onion, chopped
4 minced garlic cloves
1 chopped potato (preferably with the peel on)
2 cups water
½ teaspoon oregano (optional)
Salt to taste
Pepper to taste

Method

- Preheat butter in a small pressure cooker over medium heat.
- Sauté onion and garlic for 2 minutes.
- Add potato and sauté for 5 minutes.
- Add water. Cook over high heat till 3-4 whistles.
- Open the lid of the pressure cooker after all the air escapes.
- Blend in a juicer into a smooth soup. Add oregano, salt and pepper.
- Reheat the soup and serve with bread sticks.

Nutritive value per serving

ENERGY	FAT	CHO	C.H	FIBRE	PROTEIN	CALCIUM	IRON	VIT C
Kcal	Gm	Mg	Gm	Gm	Gm	Mg	Mg	Mg
96	4	10	14	3	2	66	1	11

76. Milk and Cream Potato

Number of servings: 4

Ingredients

10 garlic cloves
2 green chillies
4 medium sized potatoes
1 teaspoon peanut oil
Salt to taste
A pinch of turmeric powder
½ cup cream
1 cup milk

Method

- Mince garlic cloves and green chillies. Peel and cut potatoes into 4 pieces each.
- Preheat oil in a medium pressure cooker over high heat. Add garlic and green chillies and fry till they turn light brown.
- Add potatoes, salt and turmeric powder and fry for 3 minutes.
- Add cream and milk and close the lid of the pressure cooker. Simmer and cook till potatoes get tender, approximately 15-20 minutes.

Nutritive value per serving

ENERGY	FAT	CHO	C.H	FIBRE	PROTEIN	CALCIUM	IRON	VIT C
Kcal	Gm	Mg	Gm	Gm	Gm	Mg	Mg	Mg
237	11	34	30	2	6	126	1	82

77. Healthy Potato

Number of servings: 4

Ingredients

4 medium sized potatoes
2 cups yogurt
Salt to taste
A pinch of turmeric powder
2 black cardamoms
1 stick cinnamon
4 cloves

Method

- Peel and cut potatoes into 4 pieces each.
- Add all the ingredients. Transfer to a medium pressure cooker.
- Close the lid of the pressure cooker and cook over low heat till potatoes get tender, approximately 15-20 minutes.

Nutritive value per serving

ENERGY	FAT	CHO	C.H	FIBRE	PROTEIN	CALCIUM	IRON	VIT C
Kcal	Gm	Mg	Gm	Gm	Gm	Mg	Mg	Mg
211	6	16	36	7	8	252	3	32

78. *Potato Chicken*

Number of servings: 8

Ingredients

4 medium sized potatoes
3 large onions
350 grams chicken cut into 8 pieces
1 cup curd
¼ teaspoon turmeric powder
½ teaspoon red chilli powder
1 teaspoon garlic paste
1 teaspoon ginger paste
1 teaspoon coriander powder
⅓ cup mustard oil
2 dry red chillies
1 teaspoon cumin seeds
2 bay leaves
2 sticks cinnamon
Salt to taste
1 cup water
1 teaspoon garam masala

Method

- Peel and cut potatoes into 2 pieces each. Cut onions into fine roundels.
- Clean chicken. Add curd, turmeric powder, red chilli powder, garlic paste, ginger paste, coriander powder and ½ tablespoon mustard oil. Mix properly. Set aside.
- Preheat remaining oil in a large frying pan. Fry the potato pieces till golden brown over high heat. Transfer to a plate.
- In the remaining oil add dry red chillies, cumin seeds, bay leaves and cinnamon sticks.
- After a minute add onion and fry till golden brown. Add chicken along with the marinade and cover and cook over medium heat. Stir in between.
- When chicken is half done add fried potatoes and salt. Cover and cook till chicken and potatoes are tender.
- Add water and bring to a boil. Simmer for 5 minutes. Add garam masala. Remove from fire.

Nutritive value per serving

ENERGY	FAT	CHO	C.H	FIBRE	PROTEIN	CALCIUM	IRON	VIT C
Kcal	Gm	Mg	Gm	Gm	Gm	Mg	Mg	Mg
250	15	33	21	4	9	103	3	53

79. Potato Fish

Number of servings: 8

Ingredients

- 4 medium sized potatoes
- 1 onion
- 2 tomatoes
- 400 gram fish cut into 8 pieces
- 1 teaspoon turmeric powder
- ½ teaspoon red chilli powder
- 2 teaspoons garlic paste
- Salt to taste
- 2/3 cup mustard oil
- ½ teaspoon black mustard seeds
- 2 dry red chillies
- 2 bay leaves
- 1 tablespoon mustard paste/powder
- 2 cups hot water
- ½ cup chopped coriander leaves

Method

- Peel and cut potatoes into 2 pieces each.
- Chop onion and tomatoes and grind into a smooth paste.
- Clean the fish and add ½ teaspoon turmeric powder, ¼ teaspoon red chilli powder, 1 teaspoons garlic paste and salt to taste. Add potatoes. Mix well.
- Preheat oil in a large frying pan over high heat. Fry fish pieces 4 at a time till golden brown. Remove excess oil on an absorbent paper.
- In the remaining oil fry potatoes 4 pieces at a time, till they get golden brown.
- Add black mustard seeds, dry red chillies and bay leaves to the remaining oil. After a minute add onion and tomato paste, remaining turmeric powder, red chilli powder, garlic paste and mustard paste/powder
- Fry till fat leaves the sides. Add water and salt and cover and cook potatoes till they get tender.
- Add fish and simmer for 5 minutes. Remove from fire. Garnish with coriander leaves. Serve with cooked rice.

Nutritive value per serving

ENERGY	FAT	CHO	C.H	FIBRE	PROTEIN	CALCIUM	IRON	VIT C
Kcal	Gm	Mg	Gm	Gm	Gm	Mg	Mg	Mg
238	19	0	17	2	3	40	2	66

80. Potato Spread

Number of servings: 6

Ingredients

2 small sized potatoes, boiled
1½ cups milk
½ cup boiled corns
½ cup grated coconut
Salt to taste
Pepper to taste
6 bread slices

Method

- Peel and mash potatoes.
- Preheat milk in a small frying pan. Add potatoes.
- Cover and cook till the milk and potato turn into a thick paste.
- Add corns, coconut, salt and pepper. Mix well. Remove from fire.
- Toast the breads. Spread the potatoes evenly over the breads. Serve.

Nutritive value per serving

ENERGY	FAT	CHO	C.H	FIBRE	PROTEIN	CALCIUM	IRON	VIT C
Kcal	Gm	Mg	Gm	Gm	Gm	Mg	Mg	Mg
171	5	9	26	2	6	104	1	10

81. Potato Pudding

Number of servings: 2

Ingredients

2 boiled potatoes
2 cups milk
2 teaspoons sugar
½ cup boiled corns
¼ cup chopped cashew nuts

Method

- Peel and grate the potatoes. Divide into 2 equal portions and transfer to 2 different serving bowls.
- Boil milk over high heat and add sugar, corns and cashew nuts. Simmer for 3 minutes.
- Remove from fire and pour equally over the potatoes. Serve hot.

Nutritive value per serving

ENERGY	FAT	CHO	C.H	FIBRE	PROTEIN	CALCIUM	IRON	VIT C
Kcal	Gm	Mg	Gm	Gm	Gm	Mg	Mg	Mg
516	25	37	63	6	16	353	2	18

82. *Honey Potato*

Number of servings: 5

Ingredients

4 boiled potatoes
3 chopped green chillies
8 garlic cloves, minced
Salt to taste
¼ lemon
²/₃ cup honey
1 cup breadcrumbs
4 tablespoons peanut oil

Method

- Peel and mash the potatoes
- Add green chillies, garlic, salt and lemon juice. Mix well.
- Divide into 5 equal portions and make balls. Press between palms to shape into round cutlets.
- Dip the cutlets in honey. Roll in breadcrumbs.
- Preheat a griddle over high heat. Sprinkle half the oil.
- Cook the cutlets over medium heat till the underside turns golden brown.
- Turn to the other side, add remaining oil and cook till the other side turns golden brown too. Serve hot.

Nutritive value per serving

ENERGY	FAT	CHO	CH	FIBRE	PROTEIN	CALCIUM	IRON	VIT C
Kcal	Gm	Mg	Gm	Gm	Gm	Mg	Mg	Mg
515	19	3	85	4	7	110	2	79

83. Tea Flavored Potatoes

Number of servings: 4

Ingredients

4 potatoes
2 tea bags
8 cups water
2 tablespoons butter
1 tablespoon coriander seeds
2 finely chopped onions
4 slit green chillies
Salt to taste
Pepper to taste
½ lemon
1 teaspoon garam masala
½ cup chopped coriander leaves

Method

- Peel and cut potatoes into 6 pieces each.
- Add tea bags to the water. Boil the water. Add potatoes and boil till they are tender. Drain and reserve ½ cup water.
- Preheat butter in a medium frying pan over high heat. Add coriander seeds.
- After a minute add onion and fry till golden brown.
- Add potatoes, green chillies, salt and pepper. Fry over high heat for 5 minutes.
- Add lemon juice and garam masala and ½ cup reserved water. Cover and cook till water almost dries up.
- Garnish with coriander leaves.

Nutritive value per serving

ENERGY	FAT	CHO	C.H	FIBRE	PROTEIN	CALCIUM	IRON	VIT C
Kcal	Gm	Mg	Gm	Gm	Gm	Mg	Mg	Mg
206	7	16	35	4	5	89	4	161

84. Potatoes and Eggs

Number of servings: 4

Ingredients

3 medium sized potatoes
2 small onions
6 teaspoons peanut oil
4 eggs
Salt to taste
Pepper to taste
1 teaspoon cumin seeds
½ teaspoon red chilli powder

Method

- Peel and finely chop potatoes. Finely chop onions.
- Preheat 2 teaspoons oil in a small frying pan over high heat. Add half the onion. Fry till light brown.
- Break and whip the egg. Add to the fried onions.
- Add salt and pepper. Fry over high heat for 5 minutes. Transfer to a plate.
- In the same frying pan add remaining oil. Add remaining onion and fry till brown.
- Add potatoes and salt. Fry over high heat till potatoes are tender and crisp.
- Add pepper, red chilli powder and cooked eggs. Fry for 2 minutes. Serve.

Nutritive value per serving

ENERGY	FAT	CHO	C.H	FIBRE	PROTEIN	CALCIUM	IRON	VIT C
Kcal	Gm	Mg	Gm	Gm	Gm	Mg	Mg	Mg
221	11	187	22	3	8	44	2	22

85. Potato and Fish Cutlets

Number of servings: 6

Ingredients

3 boiled potatoes
200 grams boiled fish (boneless)
½ cup grated cheese
3 chopped green chillies
1 tablespoon grated ginger
8 garlic cloves, minced
Salt to taste
White pepper to taste

Method

- Peel and mash the potatoes. Mash the fish.
- Mix together potatoes, fish, cheese, green chillies, ginger, garlic, salt and pepper. Divide into 6 equal portions.
- Make oval and smooth cutlets.
- Grill in a preheated oven till the cutlets turn golden brown on both the sides. Serve hot.

Nutritive value per serving

ENERGY	FAT	CHO	C.H	FIBRE	PROTEIN	CALCIUM	IRON	VIT C
Kcal	Gm	Mg	Gm	Gm	Gm	Mg	Mg	Mg
94	trace	14	15	2	8	22	1	68

86. *Stuffed Eggs*

Number of servings- 12

Ingredients

6 hard-boiled eggs
1 small boiled potato
½ teaspoon grated ginger
½ teaspoon chilli sauce
Salt to taste
Pepper to taste
1 tablespoon tomato sauce
2 tablespoons minced coriander leaves

Method

- Shell the eggs and cut each egg into 2 pieces, lengthwise.
- Remove the yoke and keep aside.
- Peel and mash the potatoes.
- Mix yokes of 3 eggs to mashed potatoes, Add ginger, chilli sauce, salt and pepper.
- Put this mixture in equal portions in the egg whites with the help of a spoon.
- Arrange the eggs on a serving tray. Sprinkle tomato sauce over each egg piece.
- Garnish with coriander leaves and then with the remaining mashed yolk.

Nutritive value per serving

ENERGY	FAT	CHO	C.H	FIBRE	PROTEIN	CALCIUM	IRON	VIT C
Kcal	Gm	Mg	Gm	Gm	Gm	Mg	Mg	Mg
48	3	106	2	trace	3	17	1	4

87. Potato Pizzas

Number of servings: 8

Ingredients

2 boiled potatoes
Salt to taste
White pepper to taste
2 small onions
2 pizza crusts
4 teaspoons pizza sauce
2 cups grated cheese (mozzarella or cheddar)
1 tablespoon oregano

Method

- Peel and finely chop the potatoes. Add salt and pepper.
- Cut the onion into very thin roundels.
- Spread pizza sauce over the pizza breads.
- Spread the onion roundels equally over the pizza sauce.
- Spread half of the potatoes equally over the onion.
- Spread grated cheese equally.
- Finally spread the remaining potatoes over the cheese.
- Sprinkle oregano.
- Cook in a preheated oven till the cheese melts and settles properly and the potatoes on top turn brown.
- Cut each pizza into 4 portions and serve hot

Nutritive value per serving

ENERGY	FAT	CHO	C.H	FIBRE	PROTEIN	CALCIUM	IRON	VIT C
Kcal	Gm	Mg	Gm	Gm	Gm	Mg	Mg	Mg
365	5	0	67	1	11	17	1	8

88. Biscuit Chaat

Number of servings: 12

Ingredients

1 medium sized boiled potato
¼ cup grated carrot
¼ cup finely chopped parsley
4 garlic cloves, minced
⅓ cup half melted cheese
12 salted biscuits

Method

- Peel and finely chop the potato.
- Add carrot, coriander leaves, garlic and cheese. Mix well.
- Spread evenly over the biscuits, Serve immediately.

Nutritive value per serving

ENERGY	FAT	CHO	C.H	FIBRE	PROTEIN	CALCIUM	IRON	VIT C
Kcal	Gm	Mg	Gm	Gm	Gm	Mg	Mg	Mg
73	1	0	14	1	2	9	1	4

89. Potato Kebabs

Number of servings: 4

Ingredients

4 medium sized potatoes
100 grams cottage cheese
2 capsicums
2 ½ tablespoons yogurt
2 teaspoons gram flour
1 teaspoon red chilli powder
Salt to taste
1 teaspoon ajwain
2 drops edible orange color (optional)
8 teaspoons butter

Method

- Peel and cut potatoes into cubes. Boil till they are half tender. Remove from fire. Drain water.
- Cut cottage cheese and capsicums into equal sized cubes.
- Mix together yogurt, gram flour, red chilli powder, salt, ajwain and edible orange color.
- Add to potatoes, cottage cheese and capsicums. Mix well and marinate for at least 45 minutes.
- Arrange on 4 skewers and grill, basting with melted butter at least twice till they turn brown. Serve hot with onion roundels and lemon.

Nutritive value per serving

ENERGY	FAT	CHO	C.H	FIBRE	PROTEIN	CALCIUM	IRON	VIT C
Kcal	Gm	Mg	Gm	Gm	Gm	Mg	Mg	Mg
215	9	24	28	3	7	47	1	78

90. *Coriander Flavored Potato Tikka*

Number of servings: 4

Ingredients

3 large potatoes
1 bunch coriander leaves
2 green chillies
Salt to taste
2½ tablespoons yogurt
1 onion
½ lemon

Method

- Peel and cut potatoes into cubes. Half boil Remove from fire. Drain water.
- Remove coriander leaves from the stem. Grind coriander leaves and green chillies into a smooth paste.
- Add to the potatoes. Add salt and yogurt. Mix well.
- Cook in a preheated oven till potatoes are done.
- Cut onion into very thin roundels. Spread over the potatoes. Add lemon juice. Serve.

Nutritive value per serving

ENERGY	FAT	CHO	C.H	FIBRE	PROTEIN	CALCIUM	IRON	VIT C
Kcal	Gm	Mg	Gm	Gm	Gm	Mg	Mg	Mg
100	1	1	22	2	3	35	1	81

91. *Potato Rice*

Number of servings: 2

Ingredients

2 medium sized boiled potatoes
1 teaspoon mustard oil
6 garlic cloves, minced
1 dry red chilli
½ teaspoon cumin seeds
Salt to taste
2 cups cooked, hot rice
½ tablespoon ghee

Method

- Peel and mash the potatoes.
- Preheat oil in a big ladle over medium heat. Add garlic, broken red chillies and cumin seeds. Remove from fire after the dry red chillies get crisp.
- Add to the potatoes. Mix well so that the dry red chillies get completely crushed. Add salt.
- Divide potato into 8 equal portions and make balls. Set aside.
- Transfer cooked, hot rice to a plate. Sprinkle ghee.
- Add potato balls and serve immediately.

Nutritive value per serving

ENERGY	FAT	CHO	C.H	FIBRE	PROTEIN	CALCIUM	IRON	VIT C
Kcal	Gm	Mg	Gm	Gm	Gm	Mg	Mg	Mg
537	15	13	92	6	10	100	2	70

92. Stuffed Tomatoes

Number of servings: 2

Ingredients

2 large sized tomatoes
1 onion
2 green chillies
2 tablespoons peanut oil
½ teaspoon black mustard seeds
1 large boiled potato
Pepper to taste
1 teaspoon ground cumin powder
Salt to taste
¼ cup chopped coriander leaves
1 tablespoon butter

Method

- Cut a very thin slice of each tomato, on the top. Take out the pulp carefully and chop finely.
- Finely chop onion and green chillies.
- Preheat oil in a small frying pan over high heat. Add black mustard seeds.
- After half a minute add onion and green chillies and fry till golden brown.
- Peel and mash the potatoes and add to the onion along with pepper, ground cumin powder and salt.
- Fry for 3 minutes over high heat.
- Add chopped tomato pulp and fry for another 5 minutes. Add half of the coriander leaves. Remove from fire.
- Grease inside and outside of the tomato shells with butter. Fill in the prepared filling with a spoon.
- Cook in a preheated oven for 10 minutes or till tomatoes get tender. Garnish with the remaining coriander leaves.

Nutritive value per serving

ENERGY	FAT	CHO	C.H	FIBRE	PROTEIN	CALCIUM	IRON	VIT C
Kcal	Gm	Mg	Gm	Gm	Gm	Mg	Mg	Mg
301	21	16	23	5	5	90	4	169

93. Vermicelli Potato

Number of servings: 2

Ingredients

2 boiled potatoes
2 tablespoons peanut oil
1 teaspoon black mustard seeds
2 sprigs curry leaves
4 slit green chillies
1 chopped onion
½ cup green peas
3 cups thick vermicelli
2 cups water
Salt to taste

Method

- Peel and chop potatoes into 6 pieces each.
- Preheat oil over high heat in a medium frying pan.
- Add black mustard seeds, curry leaves and green chillies.
- After half a minute add onion and fry till brown.
- Add potatoes and fry over high heat till they turn reddish.
- Add green peas and fry for 2 minutes.
- Add vermicelli and fry till the vermicelli start turning brown.
- Add water and salt. Keep on stirring till all the water dries up. Serve hot

Nutritive value per serving

ENERGY	FAT	CHO	C.H	FIBRE	PROTEIN	CALCIUM	IRON	VIT C
Kcal	Gm	Mg	Gm	Gm	Gm	Mg	Mg	Mg
870	15	0	164	6	21	14	6	260

94. *Potato and Cream Balls*

Number of servings: 6

Ingredients

4 boiled potatoes
½ cup cream
Salt to taste
White Pepper to taste
¼ teaspoon red chilli powder

Method

- Peel and mash the potatoes.
- Mix all the ingredients. Make 6 equal sized balls.
- Press the balls slightly between palms and grill till brown. Serve hot.

Nutritive value per serving

ENERGY	FAT	CHO	C.H	FIBRE	PROTEIN	CALCIUM	IRON	VIT C
Kcal	Gm	Mg	Gm	Gm	Gm	Mg	Mg	Mg
197	11	20	24	3	3	55	trace	9

95. Potato Crispies

Number of servings: 4

Ingredients

2 large potatoes
1 cup rice flour
water
Salt to taste
¼ teaspoon turmeric powder
½ tablespoon white pepper
½ tablespoon garlic paste
4 half slit green chillies
1 cup peanut oil

Method

- Peel and cut potatoes into thin stripes.
- Make a batter of rice flour and water.
- Add salt, turmeric powder, white pepper and garlic paste.
- Dip potatoes and green chillies in the batter.
- Preheat oil in a small frying pan over high heat.
- Fry potatoes and green chillies over medium heat until red and crisp in 2-3 batches. Serve hot.

Nutritive value per serving

ENERGY	FAT	CHO	C.H	FIBRE	PROTEIN	CALCIUM	IRON	VIT C
Kcal	Gm	Mg	Gm	Gm	Gm	Mg	Mg	Mg
375	19	0	48	3	5	22	1	122

Note – approximately only 1/3 cup peanut oil will get used.

96. *Kashmiri Aloo*

Number of servings: 12

Ingredients

12 medium sized potatoes
1 ½ cups cream
1 tablespoon fennel powder
1 cup cashew paste
Salt to taste
½ teaspoon nutmeg powder
1 teaspoon garam masala

Method

- Peel, and boil the potatoes till they are ¾ tender. Transfer to a pressure cooker.
- Add cream, fennel powder, cashew nut paste, salt, nutmeg powder and garam masala.
- Close the lid of the pressure cooker and cook till potatoes are done.

Nutritive value per serving

ENERGY	FAT	CHO	C.H	FIBRE	PROTEIN	CALCIUM	IRON	VIT C
Kcal	Gm	Mg	Gm	Gm	Gm	Mg	Mg	Mg
233	13	26	26	3	5	41	1	24

97. Jhuri Bhaja

Number of servings: 2

Ingredients

2 potatoes
1 cup peanut oil
Salt to taste

Method

- Peel and cut each potato into very thin roundels. Cut the roundels lengthwise into pieces, as thin as possible or grate the potatoes in a grater with thick blades.
- Preheat oil in a small frying pan. Deep-fry the potatoes till they turn crisp.
- Remove from fire. Drain excess oil on a kitchen paper. Add salt.

Nutritive value per serving

ENERGY	FAT	CHO	C.H	FIBRE	PROTEIN	CALCIUM	IRON	VIT C
Kcal	Gm	Mg	Gm	Gm	Gm	Mg	Mg	Mg
335	27	0	22	2	3	9	1	24

Note – approximately, only 1/4 cup peanut oil will get used.

98. *Fried Potatoes with Rice*

Number of servings: 2

Ingredients

2½ tablespoons peanut oil

1 teaspoon cumin seeds

1 chopped onion

1 large, finely chopped potato

2 slit green chillies

2 cups cooked rice

Salt to taste

Pepper to taste

¼ cup chopped coriander leaves

Method

- Preheat oil over high heat in a medium frying pan.
- Add cumin seeds. After half a minute add onion and fry till brown.
- Add potatoes and green chillies and fry till potatoes get tender.
- Add rice, salt and pepper and fry for 5 minutes.
- Transfer to plates. Garnish with coriander leaves and serve hot.

Nutritive value per serving

ENERGY	FAT	CHO	C.H	FIBRE	PROTEIN	CALCIUM	IRON	VIT C
Kcal	Gm	Mg	Gm	Gm	Gm	Mg	Mg	Mg
3163	272	0	170	6	17	130	11	145

99. Potato Butter Masala

Number of servings: 12

Ingredients

12 small sized potatoes
6 tablespoons butter
2 black cardamoms
6 cloves
2 chopped onions
3 finely chopped tomatoes
1 tablespoon garlic paste
3 cups water
Salt to taste
½ teaspoon red chilli powder
½ cup grated coconut
2 tablespoons cashew nut paste
½ tablespoon garam masala

Method

- Peel the potatoes.
- Preheat 4 tablespoons butter in a heavy bottomed, medium sized pan over high heat.
- Add black cardamoms and cloves. After a minute add onion and fry for 3 minutes.
- Add tomato and garlic paste. Fry for 5 minutes.
- Add 1 cup water, salt and red chilli powder and potatoes. Cover and simmer till all the water dries up.
- Add coconut, cashew nut paste and 1 cup water. Cover and simmer till water almost dries up.
- Add the 3rd cup of water and cook over medium heat till the potatoes get tender.
- Add garam masala and remaining butter. Add more water if more gravy is required.

Nutritive value per serving

ENERGY	FAT	CHO	C.H	FIBRE	PROTEIN	CALCIUM	IRON	VIT C
Kcal	Gm	Mg	Gm	Gm	Gm	Mg	Mg	Mg
243	13	16	31	6	4	47	2	35

100. Potato Kulbey

Number of servings: 6

Ingredients

- 6 potatoes
- ½ cup peanut oil
- 50 grams cottage cheese
- 2 green chillies
- 6 cashew nuts
- ¾ teaspoon grated ginger
- Salt to taste
- ½ bunch coriander leaves
- 8 garlic cloves
- ¼ cup peanuts
- ½ cup yogurt

Method

- Peel the potatoes and make barrel shapes.
- Preheat oil in a medium frying pan and deep-fry the potatoes over medium heat till they are ¾ tender.
- Remove from fire and drain excess oil on a kitchen paper. Scoop out the center leaving around ¼ inch from the sides.
- Grate the cottage cheese, finely chop the green chillies and crush the cashew nuts.
- Mix cottage cheese, green chillies, cashew nuts, ginger and salt. Stuff the scooped potatoes.
- Remove coriander leaves from the stems. Grind together coriander leaves, garlic, peanuts and a little salt into a very smooth paste. (Use a few teaspoons yogurt while grinding)
- Add the paste to the remaining yogurt. Mix well. Coat stuffed potato with the yogurt.
- Cook the potatoes in a preheated oven till potatoes get completely cooked. Serve hot.

Nutritive value per serving

ENERGY	FAT	CHO	C.H	FIBRE	PROTEIN	CALCIUM	IRON	VIT C
Kcal	Gm	Mg	Gm	Gm	Gm	Mg	Mg	Mg
992	76	3	64	11	28	110	7	63

Note – approximately, only 1/4 cup peanut oil will get used.